How
MAN MADE MUSIC

To the weird accompaniment of bone clappers and gourd rattles, the Pueblo Indians of New Mexico chant their sacred prayer for rain. Like ourselves, they find that music expresses their deepest hopes and fears.

HOW MAN MADE

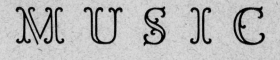

MUSIC

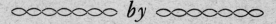 *by*

FANNIE R. BUCHANAN

*Author of Magic Music . . . Formerly Educational Specialist,
RCA Victor Staff. Now Extension Assistant, Iowa State College*

ILLUSTRATED BY

Roby Ann Nelson

WILCOX & FOLLETT CO.

1944

MUSIC

It is interesting to turn back the pages of history for thousands of years and find that no matter how far back we go music had a part in the culture of the times. Not our music, to be sure, but a music that undoubtedly reflected the spirit of the people.

It is even more interesting to turn back the pages of history to discover the ancestors of our modern instruments, to explore the growth of great musical ideas, to find the first expression of our melodies. That much in music is so little appreciated and enjoyed may be due to the very lack of this background.

But HOW MAN MADE MUSIC is more than history: it tells about Stradivarius and his famous violins and how Dan Emmett wrote *Dixie*. It brings bards, troubadours, and cloistered monks to show how music was made. It traces oratorio from a group of singing boys of Italy in the year 1600 to the famous

Handel and his *Messiah,* opera from an Italian wedding of the same year to Wagner and his great music dramas.

All this and much more is told in simple, direct language which makes HOW MAN MADE MUSIC fascinating reading and an invaluable text for beginning music history and music appreciation courses.

Many of the songs mentioned throughout the book are included in the final chapter, together with their Victor record numbers.

FANNIE R. BUCHANAN

Grinnell, Iowa.

ACKNOWLEDGMENTS

The story of the *Mysterious Voice* is revised from its original telling in *Child Life Magazine* of March, 1924. The incidents of the later life of Dan Emmett as related in the *Story of Dixie* are personal reminiscences of Dr. A. B. Graham of the U. S. Dept. of Agriculture. The newspaper clippings cited in the *Story of the Messiah* are quoted from *The Story of Oratorio* by Annie Patterson. Miss Myrtle E. Parkes, Principal of Cooper School, Grinnell, Iowa; Mr. and Mrs. H. W. Matlack of Grinnell College; and Miss Barbara A. Bates of Grinnell, have given unstinted help and suggestions in matters pertaining to grade level for school use, research and preparation.

CONTENTS

LIST OF ILLUSTRATIONS

The only musical sounds man heard were those made by the wind and waters, and by singing birds and insects

CHAPTER I

FROM SHOUTING TO SONG

(MAN BEGINS TO SING)

MUSIC has a brave story. It has made its home in palace and in cabin. It has marched with soldier and with slave. It has sailed the high sea with pirate and with Pilgrim father. Music has strange power. The song of the shepherd boy David cured the illness of King Saul when all the physicians of the realm had failed. Richard the Lion-Hearted, ill and imprisoned in a foreign land, was discovered and restored through the singing of his favorite court musician. The French national song, the *Marseillaise,* has led the troops to victory on many a hard fought battle field.

What power has music?

Music belongs to everybody. The washwoman sings at her tub, the man of affairs

1

whistles on his yacht; mayor and mechanic play in the same band; rich and poor dance to the same tunes. Wise men say there is a "music of the spheres" to which the stars and the sun and the moon all move. The song of the morning stars singing together is too fine and high for mortal ears. How then did man begin to make music? For somewhere, way back in the beginning of things, long before man learned to keep records, he learned to sing and to make songs.

From whom did early man think music came?

Legend and myth from ancient Egypt, China, India and Greece show that from earliest times people believed music to be a gift from their gods. There was a mystery about it which they could not understand. There was mystery too in the sunshine, in the winds and in the moonlight which was all about them but which they could not touch or hold! These they believed were gifts from their gods to make them happy. Music was even nearer than the sunshine. It came from within them. It expressed feelings they could not put into words.

It, too, was a gift from their gods. Through all the centuries it has been so, for even today when every school boy knows how sunlight and moonlight are made, music which comes from within, and which still expresses what can not be expressed in words, has come to be called the Divine Art. The Story of *How Man Made Music* must tell how man developed this gift of God until it became the Divine Art: how he made many different kinds of songs and instruments that each might help to express his deepest thought and emotions.

Some of this story must be guessed from the music of tribes still living in very primitive conditions in remote and undeveloped parts of the world. These tribes have war songs which to the trained ears today sound like barbaric yelling. They sing chants, using only two or three tones which are repeated over and over again like the droning song of a locust. These remote people are still using hollow reeds or conch shells for musical instruments and are still beating upon hollow stumps for drums.

How may we know about music of early times?

They dance to the sound of clappers made of wood or stone.

The story of *How Man Made Music* must trace the drums, the horns, the flutes, and the strings of the school orchestra back to just such early beginnings. It must show how organ, harp, and piano developed as man's abilities developed. A part of the story must tell how the band that plays for the football game developed from primitive stump beaters and stone clappers. Best of all it must prove how music helped to make man finer; how, as his early shouting changed to singing, his nature, too, was changing.

Where does the story of music begin?

The story begins with the making of melodies. How did man happen to make a tune? When the first builders made their crude houses they got their ideas by looking at arching caves and tree boughs. The first primitive artist drew wild animals which he saw about him. The first painter, in his sign language, saw and copied things which he wished to represent. But the first maker of tunes had nothing visible from which he might copy.   The only musical sounds he had ever heard were those made by the wind and water, and by the singing birds and insects.   These sounds were constantly moving.   The music made by primitive man must move also.   A tune cannot be stopped or held for examination.   The moment a tune is not in motion it is no longer a tune.   A brook when it stops flowing becomes a pond.   A tune when it stops moving or flowing becomes a noise.   A tune is made of sounds which move with rhythm and melody.   A noise is sound without rhythm or melody.

What is the difference between noise and music?

The early tribesman began to change noise into music when he used his hollow stump drum to give signals, because for these he must use rhythm.   He must have worked out a signal code using strong and weak beats.   Perhaps a strong beat followed by a weak beat, like this: STRONG-weak, STRONG-weak, STRONG-weak, and meant BIG-beast, BIG-beast, BIG-beast. Cheerleaders today use this same rhythm: RAH-rah, RAH-rah, RAH-rah, JOHN-son!

When the tribesman struck his hollow stump like this: STRONG-weak-weak, STRONG-weak-weak, STRONG-weak-weak, perhaps he meant EL-e-phant, EL-e-phant, EL-e-phant. The cheerleader uses this rhythm also: RAH-rah-rah, RAH-rah-rah, RAH-rah-rah, DICK-in-son!

What makes rhythm?

It is such regular repetitions of strong beats contrasted with weak beats which make the difference between cheering and mob-yelling. Such regular repetition of accents gives rhythm to any sound. Rhythm is a necessary part of all music. Rhythm is the heartbeat of music.

But a tune has melody as well as rhythm. The RAH-rah-rah of the cheerleader moves from accent to accent and is all on the same tone. A melody moves from accent to accent but it also moves from tone to tone. The familiar song, *MY*-coun-try, *TIS*-of-thee, *SWEET*-land-of, *LIB*-er-ty, moves from tone to tone and makes the melody for one of the world's best-known songs.

Now of course savage men thought nothing

about rhythm or melody. They shouted war songs as defiant as the roar of a jungle lion. They sang death chants as wailing as the moan of autumn winds. They made love songs as wistful as the call of a bird to its mate. Perhaps the first songs did really begin when men "shouted for joy" over the capture of some fierce beast of prey, or some tribal enemy. When the story of the capture was told about the campfire, perhaps the shouts were repeated and finally grew into a sort of chanted refrain. The first war songs may have started with shouts of defiance to encourage the warriors. These also may have been repeated about the campfire by the listeners, thus making the stories still more interesting.

What emotions may have first prompted song?

The early people liked such story hours. Legends of long ago describe men who made a business of storytelling. Until the time when books were made and man learned to read, these storytellers were the world's only historians. The tales they told were repeated for many generations. They became mixed with myths and legends. Some of these stories, myths, and legends have been handed down to our own time and now they are about the only records we have of what happened in those half forgotten ages. As men banded together and formed kingdoms, the storytellers, or bards as they were called, became even more important. They remembered or made up long stories. They tried to tell these in the most entertaining way possible because their living depended upon gifts from their listeners. The bards made their stories into poems or "lays." These they sang to the accompaniment of a harp.

Who were the bards?

These singing storytellers were also called minstrels. In a world without radio, newspaper, telephone, mail, movie, book, or music, a minstrel was the most welcome guest that could knock at a castle gate. Every person in the establishment from the Prince to the goatherd came to greet him. All assembled in the great hall to listen to his tales.

Even during warfare a minstrel was freely

admitted to any camp. His songs and his harp were his passport. Many good spy stories come from those days. One of the best is about King Alfred the Great. Disguised as a harper, he was admitted to the camp of the Danes. He was allowed to wander freely through the camp. When he had the information that he wanted he wandered out of the camp still singing his "lay." He left with his harp but he returned with his men and his sword and drove the Danes out of England.

Bards carried news and opinions about like a newspaper. They became very important. An old story of the British Isles shows how highly they were regarded. It tells that a king may have seven colors in his dress, a bard six, lords and ladies five, governors of a fortress four, gentlemen three, soldiers two, and the common folk might wear only one color. The Highland plaids of the Scots are said to be an outgrowth of this old way of telling the rank of a person by the number of colors he wore.

From the early days while bards were making

What did the bards do?

story-songs, the common folk, too, were singing. They made songs for their dances, and
songs for their feasts and ceremonies.

*How did some
early songs
begin?*

Other songs began in other ways. A mother
would just naturally croon a little tune to her
baby. At some time a mother somewhere
would put words to her sleepy little tune.
When this happened, the first lullaby song was
being made.

Indian lore helps to show how early songs
began. The Indian mother in some tribes still
sings a little crooning tune. She repeats the
word *wi-um* (wē-um) over and over as she
gently rocks the birch bark to which her
papoose is bound.

The Indian sings to the dawn, to the stars,
to the rain. He has made a song for hunting,
for planting, and for harvest. He has one
about his pipe, his friend, his enemy, and even
his burial. These are old, old tribal songs
which have been passed down from father to
son for many generations. They are sung in
a manner which makes the few repeated tones

seem monotonous to modern ears. These are almost the only examples in existence of the songs of primitive man. They show how music changes as man changes.

American musicians sometimes use Indian tunes in modern compositions. But to these they always add music of their own. A mourning song of an Indian woman for her lost son is one of the themes or little tunes which MacDowell uses in his funeral march called *From an Indian Lodge*. To the Indian tune MacDowell adds chords of sad, heavy music which throb along like the slow beat of tom-toms. The Indian mother would like her song better just as she made it. But a white mother feels that MacDowell's music expresses more than the lament of one mother, it pictures the tragedy of the whole vanishing Indian race.

Two very popular songs made from Indian flute calls are *From the Land of the Sky Blue Water* by Cadman and *By the Waters of Minnetonka* by Lieurance. The words of these songs are tribal legends retold in the

How do our musicians use Indian tunes?

language of the white man. The composers of each of these songs made the flute calls longer by adding little tunes of their own. Each made the Indian call more interesting by adding tones which could not be played on an Indian flute. To the melody they fitted the harmony of an accompaniment which helps the tune and the words tell the old story.

Do Indians like our kind of music?

The Indian of today does not enjoy hearing such "made-over" music. A young brave listened to a flutist playing *By the Waters of Minnetonka*. When it was finished he grunted, and in the Indian way spoke one word, "Ruined!" He still wanted the feelings and traditions of the tribe told in music as the Indian himself had made it. The composer and the people for whom he makes music have long ago passed from the tribal stage.

The civilized man of today has more and different things to think about, and he wants more and different tones in the songs he sings. Because his life has more variety than that of primitive man, he wants his songs to have

variety.   They must be made up of two or three different melodies which will give contrast.   He associates with many people and learns to think and to act agreeably with them. He wants his songs associated agreeably with other tones in what is called harmony.   He forms large bands and orchestras because he wants music with many voices.   He makes songs with soprano, alto, tenor, and bass parts for large groups to sing together.   He no longer lives the crude life of primitive man. He is more refined in his habits and in his thoughts; his speech and his music express finer feelings.   He has passed the shouting stage and now he makes singing, not shouting, music.   He is making music to express all the beautiful, the good, the noble sentiments within his soul. Music which does this may truly be called the Divine Art.

Why is our music more complicated?

Early castanets

HOW A MODERN MAN MADE A SONG

THE STORY OF DIXIE

YOUNG Dan Emmett earned his living by being funny. He was "end-man" in a minstrel show which, long before a comedy film made people laugh, was the funniest show anywhere to be seen. The end-man was the funniest part of the show. He must tell a story in a way that would set sober sides shaking. He must dance a clog that would start even a deacon's feet a-tapping, and his banjo and bones must turn any dirge into a cakewalk.

Black-face Dan was a minstrel man

Dan Emmett could do all this and more. The foolish songs he made up for the minstrel show "walk-'round" would set the audience into such roars of laughter that the men of the troupe dubbed them the "hooray songs."

But one season Dan Emmett just couldn't be funny. He had come up from a trip through the sunny south and the cold of the north was

14

getting on his nerves. He was doing his best to amuse his New York audience and, what was more important, his manager. But sometimes he was even afraid he would lose his job. He just couldn't get a smile out of life, which was most unusual for Dan Emmett.

On one stormy Saturday night when he was feeling particularly low, the manager came to him and said, "Emmett, we'll have to have a new hooray song right away. You get one ready for rehearsal Monday morning."

One day in which to write a new song!

Monday morning! It was then late Saturday night. But the manager was not to be put off. "Monday morning for rehearsal," he insisted.

Downhearted, Dan Emmett turned toward his lodging house. The wind of the street set him shivering. With a disgusted shrug he exclaimed, "New York! Oh, I wish I was in Dixie!" As he hurried along he repeated the wish over and over to himself until without knowing it he was half singing the words in time to his hurrying footsteps.

The next morning at his window, looking

Dejected and cold, Dan returned to his lodging

down upon the cold, wet street with its hurrying crowds, he again remembered the balmy days of the southland and he again repeated, "I wish I was in Dixie." This time he said it aloud and as he said it he beat an impatient tattoo upon the rain-flecked window pane. Unconsciously he repeated the words and the tattoo, and unconsciously he fitted them to the rhythm of his quick steps of the night before— "I wish I was in Dixie!"

*He wished
he was back
in Dixie*

Days of sunshine—nights of song—in Dixie. The words were a sort of magic. The end-man forgot the cold New York street. He forgot that he had to make a new song. He was hearing the punk-a-punk of the banjo strings. He was hearing the singing Negroes. He was roaming over a sunny plantation lawn. Hooray, to live and die in Dixie!

Suddenly the end-man stopped. His lips puckered into a whistle. The hooray song! He had it! "To live and die in Dixie!" That would make a hooray song worth singing!

The rhythm of his quick steps as he had

hurried along the night before belonged with the idea, so the tune, of course, had the stirring beat of a quick step mingled with the punk-a-punk of banjos. The melody that came to Dan Emmett had the smile of the south and the swing of a New York street crowd. And so, on a bleak day in a northern city, *Dixie,* the famous song of the sunny south, was born.

On a wintry day in the North Dixie was born

Monday morning at rehearsal the men of the troupe pronounced the new song a "rouser," and the manager said, "I knew you could do it."

Monday night Dan Emmett with banjo and bones sang *Dixie* for the walk-'round, and the people cheered, just as people have ever since whenever and wherever *Dixie* is heard.

The words are nonsense, but the jolly tune has kept the song a favorite when most of the other walk-'rounds of the old days have been forgotten. The swinging melody and the dancing rhythm sets every heart beating happily, and everyone agrees with the Negro orator who once said, "*Dixie* is a chune that can git up an' walk eroun' by itself!"

"Way down south in de land ob cotton"

That was the very kind of a tune the southern bandmaster needed when the North and the South went into the war of the sixties.

Dixie became a favorite war song

But instead of being sung with banjo and bones, the tune was played by fife and drum. It made a wonderful soldier-march, and soon every man, woman, and child of the South was singing *Dixie*. It became the war cry of the southern armies.

The people of the North loved *Dixie,* too. When at last the war was over, President Lincoln knew that the jolly little tune would be a real peacemaker. He had it played often at Washington, and North and South listened with mingled smiles and tears. So *Dixie* healed deep wounds and eased old scars, and became the darling of a united nation.

But for all the fame of his song, Dan Emmett received very little money for it. He had let it go for only a small amount, so while it was selling by thousands its popularity brought him not a penny. In his old age when he could no longer work he had to live as best he could on

It became the war cry of the southern armies

gifts of food and clothing. Yet in those hard years Dan Emmett still kept his love for fun and for song. Often when a show troupe came to his home town, Mt. Vernon, Ohio, he would manage to make friends with the doorkeeper and have a free seat to hear the new songs. His happiest moment was when, as sometimes happened, *Dixie* was sung or played by the company band. It was then that the old end-man forgot his troubles and lived again the triumphs of his better days.

Dan Emmett came upon hard days

One evening as he hobbled down the village street he discovered that a company he had once known was to show that night at the opera house. It was a musical comedy and the old end-man forgot his stiff joints in his eagerness to hear the jolly songs. He had no money, but he was sure the manager would remember him, and he tottered up to the ticket window to ask for admission. But the manager was not there. A brisk young stranger shook his head, "Sorry, sir, no free seats tonight."

But something in the eyes of the old man as

he turned away caught the attention of the
ticket seller. He asked a lad standing near who
the old man might be. "That's Dan Emmett,"
the boy told him. "He used to be a comedian,
a band man, and a song writer, but his songs
never made him any money and now he's down
and out."

*His name was
still known
in the theatre*

The manager was passing and caught the
name. "Dan Emmett!" he exclaimed. "Go
bring the old gentleman back. He shall be our
guest tonight."

From the front row the stooped old man
watched and listened attentively. At each
number his eyes brightened. Yet at the close a
shade passed over his face. *Dixie* had not even
been used as an encore.

But the curtain was up again. The whole
company had assembled on the stage. They
came to the very front and turned toward Dan
Emmett. The band struck into *Dixie!*

The manager signed for Dan Emmett to rise.
How the people clapped! The stooping spine
straightened. His little hooray song, as fresh

*The old man
tottered away*

and jolly as on its first night! The trembling limbs grew steady.

The Dan Emmett who stood there was strangely different from the tottering old man who two hours before had turned away from the ticket window. The faded eyes were shining. The trembling lips smiled happily. What if people did give him food and clothing? He had given them a song—a song that would never grow old; a song that had helped to bring peace after war; a song that was the darling of his country. The bowed head lifted proudly. He was no longer Dan Emmett a poor old man, he was Dan Emmett the author and composer of *Dixie!*

An hour of triumph for Dan Emmett

CHAPTER II

FROM HOLLOW STUMP TO DRUM

(INSTRUMENTS OF PERCUSSION)

*What four kinds
of instruments
are there?*

EVERY musical instrument may be given a nickname to tell how it is played. It is either a Banger, a Blower, a Picker, or a Scraper. In a large orchestra all of these kinds are heard playing together. Here it is easy to discover in which class each instrument belongs. The drums are not the only Bangers nor the horns the only Blowers. The golden harp looks too splendid to be called a Picker, but even so, the harpist sets the strings to singing by plucking them with the fingers. Because violin strings are rubbed by the bow, even this king of instruments must answer to the nickname of Scraper.

Bangers, which properly are called percussion instruments, are probably the oldest of

22

*An Indian rattle made
of buffalo hoofs*

all because they were easily made. They had their beginning away back in the times when man was making his first crude tools. All primitive people had Bangers. They clapped pieces of wood together. They struck wood against stone. They beat hollow logs with clubs. They made rattles of dried gourds and pebbles. These different kinds of sounds were the beginning of music. They pleased the tribesman and helped him to express feelings he could express in no other way.

What kind of instrument is the oldest?

One day man discovered that striking a tightly stretched dried skin gave him another kind of sound. He began to invent drums. When he learned to work with metal, he found that by striking it he could make still another new sound. He began to make bangers of metal.

But the drum was his great invention. He probably began by covering a hollow stump with a stretched skin. Some accident must have given him this idea. How it really happened may only be guessed. Drums as large

Indian rattles

as hollow stumps and as small as toys are older than man's oldest) records.

*For what
purposes were
drums used?*

Early drums were used for giving signals or alarms. In the wild life of the jungle such a loud-voiced messenger was sure to be important. Of course the tribesman kept on trying to improve it.

The chief would want to carry the drum with him on the war path. It would frighten the enemy. It would signal his own men. A portable drum must be made. To do this perhaps he burned a hollow in a piece of log and covered it with a stretched skin. Perhaps he fastened a skin over half a dried gourd.) Perhaps he made some sort of a hoop or ring to hold a stretched skin as it is held in a tambourine. It is certain that such hand drums were used in very early times.

Drums were also used in the tribal dances, which are important events among primitive people. Instead of offering prayers many tribes perform sacred dances to their gods: sun dances when they need sunshine; rain dances when

*Portable drums of
primitive people*

The drums boomed out for the dances of primitive people—dances to bring victory, to make the land fertile, to appease the gods

they need rain; war dances before going into battle; hunting dances when they need animal meat; feast dances when they are thankful for plenty. These are called ceremonial dances. They are done to the rhythmic sound of the drum. Primitive man tried to please his god by making the best dance he could. To make a better dance he had to make a better drum.

Thousands and thousands of years have passed since the time of the booming hollow stump. Men have made drums of many shapes and sizes. Yet after all, among the old ones and the new ones, there are only three different kinds. They may have a stretched skin over a hollow shell, like the kettle drums; they may have two skins, one stretched over each end of a hollow cylinder, like the bass and the snare drums; or they may have one skin stretched over an open frame, like the tambourine. These three kinds were invented long, long ago by men whose tribes have been forgotten and whose race cannot even now be traced.

These three old kinds are now made in sev-

How many kinds of drums do we have?

Sioux Indian drum
War of 1812 drum
Drum used in 1863
Drum of the Revolution
Bass drum of U. S.
* Marine Band*

eral new ways. The kettle drum, which began with the hollow stump, is the most important. Today its body is a big kettle of shiny copper. The calfskin parchment which covers it is almost transparent. Instead of being held in place by weights or stones, as the skin of the stump drum was, it is held by a metal ring. This will tighten or loosen the parchment, and in this way the drum can be tuned to the pitch of other instruments. This is why the kettle drums are so important. They are always played in pairs, because with two drums a player who is skillful at tuning can sound any tone in the scale. The kettle drums are called the tympani.

Why are the kettle drums important?

The tribesman beat his hollow stump with a club. The tympani man has several kinds of drumsticks. He has flat-headed ones of felt with a whalebone button at the tip. He has wooden ones padded with sponge and with rubber. He knows the sound each kind will make. He can not only beat out the BOOM-boom-boom of the stump drum, but he can also

The kettle drums can be tuned

make his drum roar like lions or tremble like the bleating of a timid fawn. He can express a feeling of shuddering horror or of mystery which cannot be explained by words. Through all the past centuries how man must have worked to perfect a drum which can express such different feelings!

The bass drum, like those early tribal Bangers, does not really make music, but it helps man to express his feelings by adding rhythm to tones of other instruments. Just hearing its BOOM-boom-boom makes a person feel brave. The bass drum of olden days was very heavy. Today its large hoop-like body is made of aluminum with a skin over each end. Its weight is so slight that even a school boy can carry it to beat the steady rhythm of a marching band. Sometimes the bass drum in an orchestra helps to tell a music story by imitating thunder or a roaring cannon, although it is usually just a timekeeper.

The snare drum looks like a baby bass drum, but it has an entirely different sound. Of

What use is the bass drum?

The snare and the bass drum are in every band

course, being much smaller, it would not have such a booming voice. But size is not the secret of the snare drum's crisp rattling tones.

How is the snare drum different?

It always seems to say, "I'm excited! I'm excited! Step lively! Step lively!" The snare drummer uses two round-tipped sticks of hard wood. He plays on one end of the drum only. The other end explains the secret of its exciting voice. Some inventor once stretched two strings made of dried membrane across the lower end. When the upper end is struck, these strings (snares) vibrate against the skin of the lower end. This gives the snare drum its name and its exciting sound.

Drums can also express a feeling of gaiety. The little tambourine is the gypsy drum. It is a small wooden hoop with a skin stretched over one end. It has little metal jingles wired to the sides. In the Bible story about the children of Israel this kind of instrument is called a timbrel. Miriam, the sister of Moses, used to sing and dance to its gay, jangling sound.

Besides drums, man has made many other

musical Bangers which do not play tunes.
There are the little castanets which are only
timekeepers. But they have such a quick,
snappy sound that they make any tune more
interesting. Long ago they were tribal rattle-
bones. The name castanet is Spanish, and
means chestnut wood. In Spain the first castanets were made from the chestnut tree. The
Spanish gypsies made them after hearing the
wooden clackers, which were brought into
Spain by the conquering Moors from Africa.
They are like shells made of ebony or of box-
wood and hung together on a cord.

*What other
Bangers do
we have?*

Negroes from Africa brought rattle-bones to
America. To this day the end-man in a minstrel show is still called "the bones." His
funny songs are done to the accompaniment
of the ancestor of the spoon-shaped castanets.

The nickname Bangers surely belongs to the
cymbals. For thousands of years they have
helped the drums beat out rhythm. They look
very simple, just brass hammered into two big
slightly hollowed disks. A strap by which to

*Tambourine
castanets, and
cymbals*

grasp them is fastened to the center of each. But they are not so easily made. Man had to experiment with metal for many years before his cymbals had a bright clear tone. The Turks are said to have the best sounding cymbals.

How are cymbals played?

They never tell how they combine the metals used in making them. Although cymbals have a banging sound, man long ago discovered they should not be clashed together. Instead, the player should bring the edges together with a sliding motion. Cymbals help to make exciting music. They are heard in the music of *The Hall of the Mountain King* when the home of the Trolls is destroyed.

The gong is another instrument which does not play tunes, but helps make special kinds of music. It comes from China where it is used in temple service. It is a large thin plate made from an alloy of different metals skillfully melted together. When it is brushed or rubbed by a soft drumstick, it makes a weird mysterious sound which can be increased to a really terrifying roar.

The Chinese people have many Bangers. They use stones, metal, skin, wood and baked earth to make the most surprising musical sounds. An old legend tells that long ago a myth boy showed the Chinese Emperor how to make music from stones. He selected sixteen of a certain kind and cut and shaped them until each one sounded a different tone. He then made wonderful music by tapping them with a little mallet. The Emperor named this instrument the *king*. Regardless of how the singing stones were discovered, it is true that for more than 4,000 years the king has been a favorite instrument among the Chinese.

On what Bangers can tunes be played?

The marimba of Mexico and the xylophone of Russia may be second cousins of the king, for they are also Bangers which play melodies. These are made of carefully tuned bars of very hard wood, and, like the king, are played with a little mallet. There is a sounding box or tubes under the bars to make the tone stronger.

Instead of being made by Emperors and fairy folk, perhaps these tone-making Bangers are

A xylophone is made of tuned bars of wood

only the descendants of the wooden and the stone clappers used by ancient tribesmen. What would one of those boys of long ago think if he heard a modern xylophone play *Arkansas Traveler?*

What is a carillon?

The most loved of all Bangers are the bells of many kinds, sizes and descriptions. They are found in every country of the world. Big bells to call people to church and to school; little bells to jingle on the circus clowns' caps; middle-sized bells to hang around the neck of the bell-cow so the owner may know where to find his herd; clock bells to strike hours; buoy bells to warn sailors at sea; telephone bells, train bells, sleigh bells, doorbells, and, best of all, tower bells hung in sets which not only chime musically but upon which tunes can be played.

Such a set of bells is called a carillon. The famous carillon of the Bok Tower at Lake Wales, Florida, has 61 tuned bells. The largest one weighs 22,000 pounds, and the smallest weighs 16 pounds. The bells hang in rows,

Some of the Russian bells needed a hundred men to swing the clappers

the smaller ones at the top. They are sounded by levers moved by the bell-ringer. No wonder this is called the Singing Tower and people go there from far and near to hear the bell concerts. There are many such sets of bells in the old world. The saying, "the towers of Holland sing," has become a proverb among travelers, because almost every city of this little country has its own wonderful carillon.

In an orchestra the sound of these great sets of tuned bells is imitated by a set of tuned metal tubes called orchestra chimes. There is also a German instrument called the *glockenspiel* which sounds like a tuned set of little bells.

How can orchestras use bells?

In the music story of the "Nutcracker" the French *celesta* plays for the dance of the Sugar Plum Fairy. This instrument sounds like a fairy carillon, and looks like a baby piano. It is really a set of steel plates arranged in a tiny piano-like case. When the keys are pressed, tiny hammers strike the tuned plates of steel. One famous musician described the music as "divinely beautiful!"

"The towers of Holland sing"

When may
stringed
instruments be
called Bangers?

Who would ever call a stringed instrument a Banger? But strings may be struck as well as picked and scraped. The oldest string Banger on record is the *dulcimer* of the Old Testament stories. In a picture of an Assyrian King, who lived hundreds of years before the birth of Jesus, the dulcimer is shown hanging about his neck. One hand strikes the strings with a hammer, while the other hand is pressed against the strings to muffle or to stop the sound.

The *cembalo,* which is heard in Hungarian orchestras and in gypsy camps, is one descendant of the dulcimer. But the piano is the most famous relative of this ancient instrument. Open the wooden case and there are the strings. Press the keys, and felt hammers fly up and strike them. Look carefully and see that a felt "muffler" is there with a lever to press it against the string when the tone is to be stopped.

How the piano developed from the old-time dulcimer is a story hundreds of years long. It has to do with minstrels and monks, musicians and mechanics, kings and queens, inventors,

*The dulcimer was the ancestor
of the piano*

metal workers, and many a man with an imagination. The minstrels who wandered about from country to country carried the dulcimer and its relatives of the East to the singers of the West. The monks in the monasteries invented keyboards for their organs. Inventors and mechanics borrowed this new idea and made a clavichord (*clavis*—a key; *chord*—a string). This might be called the great-great-grandmother of the piano. Musicians complained that its tones were too soft. Inventors tried to find ways to make it stronger.

What other instrument was the ancestor of the piano?

Kings gave their aid—queens helped, too, for in those times the court concert was very important. It took the place of the movies of today. The newest musical instrument caused more excitement than the newest movie reel of today, and the court musician was as important as the greatest movie star.

At last after many experiments and many failures an Italian invented a clavichord which could play either loud or very soft music. In Italian the word for soft is *piano,* and the

The Clavichord

word for loud is *forte*. So he called his instrument the *pianoforte*.

But still men worked for more than a hundred years before the piano was perfected. They made strings of wire which could be stretched tightly. They made a frame of steel which could hold the strain of the strings. They improved the hammers, the mufflers, and the keys. They invented pedals. They made square pianos, upright pianos, grand pianos. The piano of today sounds 88 different tones. It has 243 strings. The steel frame which holds these tightly stretched strings must withstand a pull or strain of 30 tons.

What was done to improve the piano?

What would the old Assyrian king think of such a dulcimer? He would have still a greater shock if he turned the button of a modern electric player-piano. Such a wonderful instrument makes people forget entirely the pianoforte's musical nickname. But haven't all the primitive Bangers really grown up to their proper name, "Instruments of Percussion?"

An old, old bell

HOW TRIBE-BOY MADE A DRUM

A MYSTERIOUS VOICE

TRIBE-BOY did not look like the boys of today. He had long shaggy hair; his finger nails were heavy and sharp like claws; his skin was tanned and coarse, for he lived in the out-of-doors.

Instead of a suit such as boys today wear, Tribe-Boy wore the striped skin of a great snake hanging from one of his shoulders. The other tribeschildren wore skins of animals. On one was the spotted skin of a hyena; another wore the grayish-yellow skin of a jackal. Some wore short skirts of woven rushes. All were bare-legged, with sandals of hide in place of shoes.

The children of the tribe wore skins of animals for clothing

At night, the tribeschildren slept in caves. For food they ate berries and nuts and flesh of wild beasts, which the men of the tribe killed. They tore the flesh into bits with their strong fingers. They gnawed the bones with their sharp teeth.

Sometimes the tribespeople would have a feast. While the meat cooked in an open fire, the young men of the tribe would dance in a circle around it. The women of the tribe kept time for the dancers. They clapped their hands and beat sticks together. This was their only music.

Then, quite by chance, the first great drum was made and Tribe-Boy found out that it could furnish music for the dancers. This is how it came about:

The women of the tribe prepared the skins for use

The tribesmen had speared a large antelope. The tribeswomen wanted the strong skin to make sandals for the tribeschildren. With sharp stone tools they scraped off the hair. Then the skin had to be dried out. Where should they stretch it?

Near by was a big hollow stump which the tribeswomen used for a barrel. Into it they put food which they wished to keep. They covered the food with small stones to keep it safe from squirrels and other animals. That day the hollow stump was empty. Its edges

With sharp stones they scraped the hide

had become worn and smooth. It would make a good drying frame. The tribeswomen spread the skin over it, and with strong sinews they tied stone weights to the corners to hold it in place.

Day after day the sun took up the moisture from the skin. As it became dry, it grew smaller but the weights still held it. Soon it was very tight across the top of the stump.

A hollow stump made a good drying frame

One afternoon the women were roasting a wild boar. Back from the fire, the men sat around the tribal chief. The chief was very old, but he was still tall and straight. His eyes were keen and bright. The tribesmen knew that he was wise and clever. It was he alone who should wear the splendid striped skin of the jungle tiger; it was he alone, of all the tribe, who should have the bright feather of the flamingo for his head dress.

The tribeschildren were playing about the hollow stump. Tribe-Boy was with them. The tribeschildren liked his games. He was much more clever than they. He was tall and straight like the chief. Tribe-Boy was proud of his strong arm. "See," he said, "it is so that I killed the big snake!" He raised his stick for a great stroke. As it came down, it struck the tight skin across the hollow stump.

Boom! The sound echoed through the jungle!

The taut skin resounded from the blow

Tribe-Boy sprang back from the stump. The tribeschildren cried out in terror. The tribesmen and women came running to find out what the great sound might be. The children could not tell them. They pointed to the stump. They pointed to Tribe-Boy.

The old chief asked him questions. "What made the loud cry?" But Tribe-boy could only tell that the great voice had come from the hollow stump. Some strange wild creature must be hiding there. At last, to show the old chief, Tribe-Boy again brought the stick down on the stretched skin.

Boom!

The children shrieked and ran to their mothers. The men grasped their spears and clubs

The children ran to their mothers

and formed in a line between the women and the crying stump. They were sure that some fierce beast was crouching there under the skin. They stood waiting for it to spring out upon them. But the skin did not move. There was no sound from the hollow stump.

After a while the men came closer. They saw the stone weights that held the skin in place. The strange beast was trapped! Then there was great rejoicing. The young men danced to celebrate the capture of the loud voiced animal. As they passed the stump some of the most daring struck the skin to make the creature cry out. At this the children covered their ears; the old men shook their heads; the women were too frightened to clap for the dancers.

Back from the others, beside the old chief, Tribe-Boy stood watching. Suddenly he had an idea. Grasping his stick he sprang through the circle. He bounded close to the stump. He struck the skin, and the voice boomed in answer. Tribe-Boy stood his ground. He struck

They thought a wild creature was trapped

The spear men formed a line to guard the women

the skin time after time with short quick strokes, and time after time, to each stroke, the voice answered.

The men stopped their dance to watch. The children stopped their crying to listen. The eyes of the old chief followed every motion of Tribe-Boy's stick.

Tribe-Boy began to beat a rhythm on the new drum

Then Tribe-Boy began to beat in rhythm as he had heard the tribeswomen clap for the dancers. And the voice answered in rhythm, time and again, "BOOM, Boom-boom-boom! BOOM, Boom-boom-boom!"

The young men liked this. They shouted aloud and sprang into a circle-dance about the stump. The women liked it, too. They laughed and chattered and began to clap, keeping time to the booming. The children and the old men gathered about.

Suddenly the old chief sprang into the circle, leaping and bounding in time to the booming. The long tail of his tiger skin lashed his ankles, and the bright feathers of his headdress waved wildly. How the men shouted! It was long

The old chief sprang into the circle

since the old chief had danced in the circle! But now he was young again. He sprang into the air like the cliff-kids; he turned and whirled like the tree-squirrel! The tribeschildren had never seen such dancing. They clapped and stamped with their mothers. Tribe-Boy beat faster and faster.

The drum made fine music for dancing

At last the wild dance ended. The tired dancers dropped to the ground. But the old chief came to where Tribe-Boy stood beside the speaking stump. "You are very brave," he said. "You shall be the keeper of this great voice. For you it shall speak to make old hearts young, dull eyes sparkle, and heavy feet light." From his own hair he took the flamingo feather, and placed it in the matted hair of Tribe-Boy. "You are very brave," he said. "For you the voice shall speak and the people will love it."

That night, while the tribespeople slept, Tribe-Boy sat alone beside the hollow stump. If only he might see this hidden creature! "It has not moved," he said to himself. "It has not moved. It is sleeping. I must see it."

Tribe-Boy beat faster and faster

He caught up a torch from the fire and fastened it into the crotch of a tree above him. With his strong fingers he loosened the heavy weights. "I must, I must see this strange creature that speaks for the dancing—"

But there was no creature in the drum!

But when he lifted the skin, holding the torch for light, there was only the empty hollow of the stump! Then Tribe-Boy's hands trembled as the tiny fronds of the tree-fern do when the little rains touch them. His sturdy limbs shook as the tall palm does when the roaring wind sweeps the jungle. He crouched beside the empty stump.

Far off in the sky there came a flash of lightning. Tribe-Boy caught the roll of distant thunder. He lifted his head. Here, too, was a great voice. Many times he had heard it speak, yet always from the air above, where his eyes could find no creature. Was the voice of the hollow stump a child of this greater hidden voice which only spoke from behind the clouds? If he covered the stump would the booming voice speak for him again?

The stump was empty

Tribe-Boy sprang to his feet. He replaced the skin. He fastened the stone weights. At last, when the stretched skin again covered the hollow stump, Tribe-Boy seized his stick, and, half afraid, he tapped the skin gently. The voice answered softly.

Tribe-Boy made a great discovery

Tribe-Boy dropped to his knees beside the hollow stump. Throwing his arms across the stretched skin, he pressed his cheek close against it. "You are there," he cried softly, "you are there. I may not see you, but I shall keep you, and you shall speak for me, and my people shall love you!"

How the tribes found that any hollow stump or hollow bowl, if it be covered by a tightly stretched skin, will hold the voice of the drum, we may never know. There are no books old enough to tell us. But this we do know, that as the stump-drum spoke for the Tribe-Boy long ago, the drums still speak for us today. Their voices still make old hearts young, dull eyes sparkle, and heavy feet grow light; and the people still love them.

Chapter III

FROM RAM'S HORN TO TRUMPET

(How Horns Were Made)

What does the music of a horn do?

THE school band is marching up the street. Its horns of brass and of silver flash brightly in the sunlight. Its music sets the air ringing. With heads high the players step proudly. Passers-by stand to watch them. All along the street spines straighten and chins go up. The horns are calling out their age-old challenge, "Attention!" All who hear become alert. The sound of a horn has always made people stop and listen.

In the days before man learned to make bowls of clay he used an animal horn from which to drink. No story is old enough to tell when or how man first discovered that the hollow horn or tusk of a wild animal could make a startling sound. But there are very

46

ancient stories which show how these have long been used to give commanding signals. In drinking, the large end was raised to the lips. How did primitive man get the idea of turning the horn about and blowing into the small end? Perhaps the story might have been like this:

Some tribesman had an especially fine drinking horn. It was long and slender. He had polished it inside and outside by rubbing it with sand and pebbles. He prized it greatly. In some way the tip became broken. He was looking it over as a boy would examine a broken knife. By chance he put the tip to his lips and blew into it. Then came a most surprising blast of sound. From near and far the tribes people came running. What a wonderful signal! A great discovery had been made!

How might man have learned to blow a horn?

But blowing a horn is not always as easy as that. To produce horn tones the lips and the breath must be used in very special ways. That tribesman had a horn which was well shaped. He happened to press his lips into the opening in just the right way. When he blew it again, perhaps the sound did not come at all. Perhaps many days and even seasons passed before those primitive men learned which horns were best. They had to learn, too, how the lips help to make the horn signal. Yet in some way man did learn how to produce certain tones from these animal horns.

What are the notes of a horn?

The natural tones of a well shaped horn are *do, do above, sol above.* Horns which sounded these three tones were the easiest to blow. These tones became so familiar that a horn which did not produce them was considered coarse and unpleasant. Sometimes a skillful blower with an unusually long horn could sound even a fourth tone, the second *do above.* Such horns were highly prized and were passed on from generation to generation. Through hundreds of years, they became the foundation of the *do-re-mi* scale which every school boy knows.

As primitive man learned to use tools and

to work with wood and metal, he found ways
to improve his signal horn. He found that
the largest and longest horn would sound the
best signal because a long, hollow tube sounds
a better, clearer tone than a short one. He
invented mouthpieces of different shapes to fit
into the tip of his horn. These helped his lips
to make the tones stronger. He lengthened
the tube by adding other pieces of horn. This
helped him to make the tones more certain.
Using wood and metal he made horns with
very long tubes. These would sound the tone
mi above the highest *do* of the old tubes. Some
of the ancient horns were so long that when
they were used the flaring end, or bell as it is
called, had to be supported on a rack or a stand.

An old, old Bible story of the Jewish people
tells of two such horns. (Numbers, 10th chapter.) In the story they are spoken of as trumpets. Moses used them for signals while he
was guiding the children of Israel through the
wilderness into the promised land. These
signal horns were made of solid silver, and must

*How were
horns improved?*

have been very long, and have had very powerful voices. The signals were heard by the
thousands of Israelites in their camps. When
one trumpet sounded, all the princes came together in a central meeting place. When both
trumpets sounded, all the people gathered in
one assembly. The old story also explains that
when the trumpets sounded an "alarm" all the
people knew that they were to break camp and
move forward.

*What horns
did the
Israelites have?*

This story helps to prove that thousands of
years ago man had already learned to make
metal horns with which different signals could
successfully be given, although only a few tones
could be sounded.

Shepherds in mountain countries of the old
world still use wooden horns fifteen or sixteen
feet long. The flaring end, or bell, rests upon
the ground as the shepherd plays his herd call.
The tones echo down the valleys and up among
the peaks. Other shepherds hear and answer.
Each shepherd has his own call made up from
the few tones his horn can sound.

*Horns like this can be
seen today in Europe*

Even in very ancient times there were many shapes and sizes of horns. The Knights of King Arthur's Court carried ivory ones made from elephant tusks. These were called *"oliphants."* They were beautifully carved and decorated. In those days of knighthood, when there were many nobles, each with his own great estate, every landowner had his own horn call. When lands changed owners, this call was part of the formal ceremony. Villages then had a town horn in place of the town bell of today. When stage coaches came into use, the post horn was always sounded with a flourish as the coach drew up to the tavern door. These coach or post horns were much like the bugles which are now used in Drum and Bugle Corps of the grade schools. The best of them could sound *do, mi,* and *sol.*

What were some early uses of the horn?

Long ago fox hunting was a most popular sport among the aristocracy. Then every countryside had its famous hunter. Over his scarlet coat he wore his fox horn hanging by a cord about his shoulder. Hunting horns were longer and more slender than the post horns. They could sound five tones, *do, do above, sol above, do above, mi above*. Some extra long ones would even sound a higher *do*.

What did men do with extra long horns?

How could a hunter ride through the forest with such a horn swinging at his side? He managed it in this way: By experimenting he found that a tube may be curved without changing its tone. He coiled the long slender horn into a big circle through which he slipped his head and his right arm. The circle rested on his left shoulder. The flare, or bell, was behind and the mouthpiece in front, where it could be lifted easily to the lips.

Now that several tones of different pitch could be sounded from his horn, the hunter began to make different calls. Each master of the chase had his own signal by which he could tell his mates how the hunt was going. First there was the "Call to the Chase;" then the call to tell that a fresh track had been found; the "View Hallo" was sounded when the fox was sighted; the "Mort" told that the fox had been taken. There were also different calls for different animals.

All this meant that the horns were being made better. The tube had now become so long that it was worn in a double coil about the shoulders of the hunter. Because more tones could be sounded the hunters began to make up fancy calls and longer tunes to express their joy after a successful chase. In this way the horn began to make music as well as signals. It was learning to sing as well as to shout.

In the early days when two horns were used together to give one signal they were of different lengths. A shorter tube always sounds a higher tone than a long one. This is why a signal using two horns would easily be distinguished from a signal sounded on one horn. Then some clever tribesman invented a way to make his one horn sound the tones of both a long and a short tube. This is the way he did it. He cut a small hole in the side of his long horn. This had the effect of shortening the tube and made his long horn sound the

*How did men
get more notes
from a horn?*

*The fox hunter had to coil
his horn over his shoulder*

tones of a short horn. When he pressed his finger tightly over the hole and closed it, his horn gave its original tones. This was a great invention.

Why are horns curved and coiled?

Through hundreds of years man worked at this idea and improved upon it. Horns were made with as many holes as a player had fingers with which to cover them. What a lot of experimenting was required to find just where to place these useful finger holes! When at last they were located in just the right position to produce the tone wanted, the tube of the horn had to be curved and coiled to bring the holes within reach of the player's fingers. One of the old-time horns of this kind which had six finger holes was called the "serpent." In order to bring the holes within reach of the player the tube had to be curved in and out in much the shape of a wriggling snake.

All this time, and for hundreds of years after, horns were being made in many different ways. At last they were really singing instruments. Some kinds were not so good as others. The

A later form of "serpent"

poor ones would be used for a time and then
would be laid aside and forgotten as the old
serpent-horn had been. But the best kinds
were gradually made better in every way.

The greatest improvement came through the
invention of valves, which can make the tube
shorter or longer at the touch of a finger on a
key or lever. By the use of such valves the best
of the old signal horns became singing horns
and are found in the bands and orchestras of
today. These do not look at all like the first
signal horns, but if the brass tubes are uncoiled
and straightened out they are found to have
the tapering shape of the old-time animal horn.
But of course they are many times longer and
the flare is much wider than ever grew upon the
head of any animal.

*Of what use
are valves?*

The trumpet and the trombone do not have
this tapering shape. They have slender tubes
which do not flare until the abrupt spread of
the bell. For this reason they are called trumpets instead of horns.

The trumpet is the "Old Warrior" of the

The trumpet

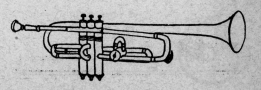

music world. All the great battles of history are in its story; all the pride of victory is in its strong, confident voice. If its slender tube were uncoiled it would need a support or stand such as was used for the famous silver trumpets of the old Bible story, for it is nine feet from tip to bell. But today war signals are given by the army bugle while the trumpet, instead of calling to battle, joins with the other instruments in helping man to make music so inspiring and so fascinating that people, as they listen, forget about fighting.

What is the difference between a trumpet and a trombone?

The Italians sometimes call the trombone the Tromba Spezzata or the "broken trumpet," because its tube is shortened by sliding one half over the other instead of using valves. They have another name for it meaning "big trumpet." These are good names, for if the trumpet and the trombone were uncoiled and placed side by side they would be alike in shape and length, but, being larger around, the trombone has a deeper sounding voice.

The old-time hunting horn is now the French

The trombone or "broken" trumpet

horn. It has a sweet, wistful voice. The name and the gentle voice came after a musician used it in his orchestra to remind his audience that his music was about a hunting party. No horn had ever before been used in a concert hall. In those days only stringed instruments were used in orchestras. Because this happened in France, the horn was ever after called the French horn. The people liked the idea of the hunting call in the music, but they thought the tones of the horn too loud and harsh. It had to be made more mellow. In doing this the tube was made longer and more flaring. Its fifteen foot length is still coiled in a circle as in its old hunting days, but it is no longer carried over the head of the player. Now its voice is haunting and far away; it is a dreamer recalling mysterious woodland haunts of long, long ago.

What is the French horn like?

The cornet is the good sport of the high school orchestra. If there is no trumpet it will take the trumpet's part and do it very well. It often has to do this because it is more easily

The cornet can take the trumpet's part

played. In shape the cornet is between a horn and a trumpet. Its voice is not so brilliant as that of the trumpet, because the tube of the cornet is more flaring. In the school band, and every other brass band, the cornet is very important. It always plays the melody.

What is the largest horn of all?

The tuba is a bass singer. If it were uncoiled and standing on its big flaring bell, a man on the top of a twelve-foot ladder could barely reach the mouthpiece. It is the largest and the longest of all brass instruments, and sounds the deepest tone. Yet for all its size, the tuba's big voice can sing smoothly and gently. It can play a very sprightly tune, too. When it does, it is not, as one might imagine, like a dancing elephant, but more like a very agile clown.

The sousaphone is another large tuba which is named after Sousa, the band master who composed *The Stars and Stripes Forever*. Its great flaring tube is circled so that it can be slipped over the head and rested on the shoulder of the player. In this way it is easily carried in marching bands. The helicon is still another kind of

The tuba is the largest of the brasses

tuba. It also is circled about the head of the player but its bell, or flare, is not so large or so open as that of the sousaphone.

The saxhorns of the school band are of different sizes. They are named for a Belgian, Charles Sax, who invented many kinds of musical instruments. He made the old-time bugles over into horns which he fitted with keys so skillfully arranged that the saxhorns can sound even more tones than the human voice. He also invented the saxophone, which has the tube of a horn but the mouthpiece of a clarinet, and belongs to the wood-wind instruments.

What great changes and inventions and improvements have been made since that first signal horn! Now all the brass instruments which developed from it can sing as well as shout. Their tones are beautiful, and yet they still have that old-time command. There is something in the sound of a horn which puts new life into tired feet and makes the heart beat faster.

Animal Horn
Early Bronze Horn
Oliphant
Hunting Horn
French Horn

CHAPTER IV

FROM PIPE TO PIPE ORGAN

(OTHER PIPES THAT SING)

*What were the
ancestors of
the flute?*

ANY boy can make a pumpkin-vine bassoon or a willow whistle. These are the ancestors of the high school orchestra's flutes and oboes. Even the great pipe organ began long, long ago when some shepherd boy played a little tune on his home-made pipes.

Man used his first tools to help him make music. In the days of the saber-tooth tiger, boys made flutes for themselves. Among the oldest relics of mankind is a little whistle made from a hollow bone. It was found in an ancient cave dwelling in France. For thousands of years it had been buried with some little flint knives such as man used before he learned to work with metals. A little bone flute with three finger holes was found in another such

60

Prehistoric bone whistle
Prehistoric flute
A much later flute
A primitive reed instrument

cave dwelling. The boy who made this must have had a few crude tools. He had found out how finger holes would help his flute to sound more tones.

There are flute myths and stories from every age and from every country. The children of ancient Egypt believed that the flute was given to them by the water-god of the river Nile. This was because their early flutes were made of river reeds or rushes.

What early people had flutes?

In those days the people of Egypt painted pictures on the walls of their tombs. One wall has a picture showing seven musicians, each playing a flute as long as a man's arm. Two flutes made from slender grass reeds were found in a tomb of one of the great pyramids.

The Hindu children of India are taught that one of their gods invented the flute for them. The Chinese have no story old enough to tell who first made their soft-toned flute from a bamboo stalk. The old myth of Pan and his pipes is told in many school readers. Almost every child knows how this god, who never grew up, bound river reeds together, and made a set of singing pipes.

America, too, has its flute story. Long before Columbus came to this country the Indian boy had found how to make a flute. He used it in wooing his Indian sweetheart. Each Indian lover made up his own particular love call.

From what country have the best flute stories come?

But the best stories come from the ancient land of Greece. There the flute was played in almost every home. A gentleman was disgraced if he could not play it. It was used in all public events, too. Chariot races and boxing matches were accompanied by flute players. The ships of Greece had trained flute players to mark the time for the rowers. There were many flute-playing contests between the different cities. The people of Thebes, an ancient city of Greece, set up a statue bearing this inscription, "Greece has declared that Thebes wins the prize upon the flute." The story is told that in one contest a player blew himself to death trying to win the prize. Some of the Greek flutes were made in pairs.

In ancient Rome a flute player wore a bright yellow dress and green or blue slippers embroidered in silver. One of the great Roman orators always kept a flute player standing back of him to sound a low tone in case he pitched his voice too high. Once the flute players of a Roman city became offended and "called a strike." They "walked out" at the time of a big festival and all went to another town. But the festival could not go on without the flute players. They were brought back, given all they had asked for, and in addition were granted three days vacation every year.

In Greek stories all slender, singing, hollow reeds and pipes were called flutes. There were long flutes and short flutes. Some were played from the end and some from the side. Also there were double flutes. Some of these were joined in one mouthpiece. There were different kinds of mouthpieces. Some had a notch cut in the end over which the player blew his breath to make the sound; some had a round hole in the side near the tip-end over which the breath

What different kinds of flutes are there?

Most primitive people have flutes of some kind

of the player was blown; some had a little thin piece, or slip, of reed fastened in the tip against which the player blew, as boys today blow through a blade of grass held tightly between their thumbs. The different kinds of pipes and mouthpieces made different kinds of tones.

Why are these instruments called wood winds?

Long before written history, man had learned how to use finger holes in his singing pipes as he used them in his signal horns. Perhaps he learned how to play a little pipe tune even before he learned to make his first horn call. However this may be, it was from his simple singing reeds and pipes that man developed the different kinds of wood-wind instruments in use today. Each one has its own particular kind of mouthpiece and its own peculiar voice. Yet the wood-wind instruments all sing of the out-of-doors, of whispering trees, of trilling birds, and of murmuring waters. Perhaps this is because they were first made by country people who played their pipes as a pleasant pastime and were made happier by their music.

But this is not the reason they were called wood-wind instruments. The name was given to them because at one time they were all made of wood. Now, although they are also made of metal, the old name still clings to them, and it still does describe their voices.

The silver flute of today is the pipe with the mouthpiece in which the breath of the player is blown across the opening instead of into the pipe. Blowing the breath across the open end of an empty bottle will show how the sound of the flute is produced.

Many men worked through many centuries to improve the flute, yet when it was played with other instruments its tones were never quite exact. Finally, about one hundred years ago, a German by the name of Boehm (bām) made one which was so nearly perfect that it became a model. When Boehm was only a boy he began to work with his flute. By the time he was fourteen years old he had made one with four finger holes. From that time on he was always trying to make a better one. At last

What was wrong with the flute?

*How was the
flute improved?*

when he was fifty-seven years old he was awarded a gold medal for having made the best flute shown at a great exhibition held in London. In making the award the judge said, "One person brings a flute with a fine note E, another with some other fine note, but what we want is a flute with all the notes equally fine, and this we find in the Boehm flute." But what years of work had been necessary to produce it! In carrying out one of his experiments Boehm had changed or remade his flute three hundred times. He had made both the tube and the mouthpiece better, but his best work was done in improving the finger holes and the keys with which they are covered.

The silver flute is the showy, fancy singer of the wood-wind group. It can play a high, clear melody and add trills and frills to rival any canary bird. It can sing a low, quiet melody such as the Indian lover played to call his Indian sweetheart.

The little brother of the flute, the piccolo, is just half as big as the flute and its voice is so

*The flute and his little
brother the piccolo*

shrill that it is called the "imp of the orchestra."
In *The Storm* music of the *William Tell Overture* the piccolo represents the shrieking wind
and the blinding flash of the lightning.

The oboe is the sweet singer of the wood-
winds. It does no fancy turns such as are done
by the flute. Its voice is so simple and friendly
it might represent a young shepherdess singing
to her flocks as she leads them through a sunny
meadow. Sometimes the oboe plays a happy
little dance tune. Then its voice is jolly. The
young shepherdess is in a group of girls and
boys doing an old-time folk dance where everybody swings everybody else.

*How is the
oboe different?*

Some people say that the oboe sings through
its nose. Its voice does have a sort of a nasal
twang which musicians describe as "reedy."
This is because its mouthpiece is made of two
little slips of reed or cane fastened into a small
metal tube which fits into the tip end of the
oboe. The player blows through these two
reeds. They vibrate together and give the
oboe a very unusual voice.

*The oboe and its sister,
the English horn*

Everybody loves the oboe and its deeper voiced sister, the English horn, which is not a horn at all. It is a larger oboe which, it is said, has developed from an old time English shepherd's pipe. Its voice is so tender and dreamy that even when it plays a shepherd's dance there is something about its voice which makes one remember the lonely life of a mountain herdsman. In the music of the *William Tell Overture* the song of the shepherd in *The Calm* is played by the English horn.

What gives the clarinet a different tone?

A pipe with still another kind of mouthpiece developed into the clarinet. It has one reed, or slip of cane, fitted into the chisel-shaped tip of the tube. In blowing, the player presses this against the lip. The vibration of the lip and the reed, and the breath in the tube all combine to give another kind of wood-wind voice. In bands the clarinets play the parts which in orchestras are played by the violins. Because its voice blends so well with other instruments the clarinet is very useful. A large band will have as many as twenty clarinets.

Both the alto and bass clarinets look like giant smoking pipes. The tube curves upward near the bell end, and the tip end is bent in toward the player. All clarinets, however, have the same chisel-shaped mouthpiece with one flat piece of reed and all have the same kind of voice.

The funny member of the wood-wind group is the bassoon. It might be called the instrument joker because its deep-toned voice is as sprightly as any tumbling clown. In the troll music of *The Hall of the Mountain King* it leads the dancing imps. In the *Midsummer Night's Dream* music it brays for the donkey and leads the clown march of the "six hard men of Athens." But in the *Nocturne (Night Song)* of this same music its voice is dignified and beautiful.

The bassoon is really a bass oboe for it has the same mouthpiece. It is an odd-looking instrument with a wooden pipe or tube about eight feet long. This is doubled or folded back upon itself to bring the finger holes within

What is a bassoon?

The Clarinet is straight but the bass Clarinet looks like a pipe

reach of the player who wears the bassoon strapped across his body diagonally and blows into a long slender tube which is needed to bring the mouthpiece within reach.

What other Blowers are there?

Besides wood-winds there are many other Blowers. There are the accordion, the concertina, and the little reed organ. These all have sets of little metal tongues or reeds which make music when struck by air blown from a bellows. The harmonica, or mouth organ, has the same kind of little metal reeds which are made to sound by the breath of the player.

The bagpipe is a very old and famous Blower. Scotland may claim its "skirling" voice but "the pipes" were "calling" in other lands long before Scottish chiefs used them to call the clans together. However, the bagpipe is built on a "Scotch" plan, three or four pipes being made to sound when only one is blown. The pipes are fitted into a leather bag in such a way that when the player blows the singing pipe, all the others also sound. These extra pipes are called the "drones" because they drone

The bassoon is really a bass oboe

along in a lower tone than the melody pipe. The instrument has had many different names. Every civilized nation since history began has known the "sackpipe," or *dudelsack* as the Germans call it.   But for hundreds of years it has been Scotland's favorite, and now whenever its shrill voice is heard the highland plaid and bonnet are sure to be close at hand.

The great cathedral organ, the grandest of all instruments, is the aristocrat of the Blowers.   Yet this most magnificent of all music makers had its humble beginnings in Pan's pipes and the droning dudelsack.   The first organ was a set of pipes placed in a "wind chest" or box in such a way that air forced into the box would sound each pipe.

One of the most interesting of all music stories would show how, step by step and through hundreds of years, this primitive instrument grew up into the splendid organ of today.   Such a story would have many funny chapters and many strange pictures, for organs, as they grew larger, were often built, blown,

The great organ started with the reed pipe

and played in very quaint ways. In old organs the wind chest had to be filled by bellows. If the bellows-blower went to sleep the music would come to a sudden stop. A cartoon almost eight hundred years old shows four bellows boys who have been loafing on the job. The organist is telling them just how he feels about it.

An organ which was built in Jerusalem fifteen hundred years ago is described as having twelve brass pipes and a wind chest made of two elephant skins which needed fifteen bellows to fill it. The old story also said this organ could be heard at the Mount of Olives which was a mile from Jerusalem.

How were the first organs played?

In the first organs the player used his hand to open or close the pipes as they were needed. There were many inventions between that time and the time when keys were used to open and close pipes. When the organ keys were first used they were so large that the organist had to strike them with his fist.

Today the organist, with his hands, plays

three or four keyboards called manuals. At the same time he plays the pedal keyboard with his feet. The wind is furnished by electric power. With a set of stops the organist can instantly change the organ tone from the wistful call of a single flute to the grand peal of a thousand deep-toned pipes.

From willow whistle to cathedral organ is a beautiful music story. Every page reveals that whether whistling reed or mighty organ, singing pipes have always been made for the pleasure, contentment, and inspiration of man.

CHAPTER V

FROM BOWSTRING TO VIOLIN

(THE HARP AND ITS CHILDREN)

FIFTY thousand dollars for a handful of wood! But the handful of wood is a magic violin. It has a magic story, too.

The story begins in the days when the hunter's bow was a part of every man's equipment. He depended upon it for his food, his clothing, and his protection from lurking foe or stalking beast.

The hunter of those times had to be sure of his bowstring. A good string on a well-bent bow always hummed as it sent the arrow flying. The hunter learned to listen for this humming sound. He noticed that long bowstrings twanged with a deeper tone than the shorter strings. He liked the sound of the short and long strings humming together.

What was the beginning of stringed instruments?

74

The bowman listened to the hum of his string

Perhaps at night about the camp fire these old-time hunters twanged the bowstrings with their fingers, just for the sake of hearing them hum. Perhaps as they sat there they made a little song to go with the humming sound. In some way the bowstrings must have been used for pleasure as well as for protection, because somewhere in those forgotten times man began to make music from stretched strings. He had learned to make drums to help with his dances. He had learned to make pipes that would sing to him when he was lonely, and help him keep his flocks from straying. Now he was to learn to sing with the strings, and afterward to find new ways to make them sing for him.

There was a long, long time, thousands of years, from the first singing strings to the magic violin. Before such an instrument could be made man must learn many secrets about singing strings. How could one string produce tones of different pitch? How could several strings be tuned to sound in harmony? How could the tones be made stronger? How

What did man have to learn about strings?

Someone thought to put two singing strings on one bow

could strings be made to play the melodies of
his songs?

What two kinds
of stringed
instruments
do we have?

These were puzzles which man was to work
out. While doing so, he discovered that
strings can sound in many different ways. He
made many kinds of stringed instruments.
Some were Pickers and some were Scrapers.
The Pickers must have been made before the
Scrapers because they were more simply constructed.

The harp was the first Picker. It probably
began when one of those early hunters, in the
arch of his bow, put a short string back of his
long string. He had ruined his bow for hunting and for fighting, but he had made the first
harp.

It would be interesting to know what tones
those first two harp strings sounded! If the
shorter string was exactly half as long as the
first string, and was exactly the same size and
kind, and if the hunter stretched it just as
tightly, it would sound the *sol* above the tone of
the first string. Very early in his experiments

*Men found they could pluck sounds from taut strings, and for
centuries minstrels carried music from court to court*

with strings man must have worked out many such puzzles. Long before written history he had found how to make strings sound certain tones.

Just as the ancient cave dwellings tell of the first flutes, so ruins of ancient cities tell of the first harps. In Babylonia a few years ago explorers discovered a buried city. Among the ruins was a slab of stone ornamented with carvings representing musicians, one of whom is seated and playing a harp with eleven strings. When this stone picture was made more than four thousand years ago, man had already learned to tune strings. He had a way of stretching them with varying tightness, for in this way strings produce tones of different pitch. All this can be certain from the picture, although it can never be known what melodies the strings sounded.

What do ancient ruins tell us about harps?

The tombs and ruins of ancient Egypt are picture galleries of the past which tell fascinating stories about music. More than four thousand years ago the Egyptians decorated the walls and columns of their great buildings with pictures and sculptures and sacred writing. Because of the dry atmosphere of Egypt, these are still preserved. Even the paintings have not lost their colors.

Processions of singers and dancers and harpers are there on the monuments. Along with these are sign stories which tell of choruses of twelve hundred singers, and orchestras of six hundred players. Things were done on a large scale in ancient Egypt!

Were all the harps carried?

These pictures show harps more than six feet high. The base, which rests on the floor, is richly decorated. Some are carved with the head of the King, and others with the great lotus flower which was such a favorite among Egyptians. The base extends upward in a bent bow shape which curves forward at the top. This board also is magnificently adorned with designs done in colors and jewels. Such harps were used in the temples. They show as many as twenty-three strings.

There are also pictures of smaller harps.

The Egyptians made elaborate harps

Some have three strings and are being played as they are carried, resting upon the shoulder in an almost horizontal position. All the Egyptian harps were without the front pillar which is so important in harps of the present time. But their form plainly suggests the curve of the old hunting bow.

In all ancient harps, this bow had been very greatly broadened, which proves that four thousand years ago man had already worked out another of the puzzles. He had found how to make the tones stronger by using a board which vibrated with the strings. Such a device is called a soundboard.

What was the soundboard?

While experimenting with the harp, man made other stringed instruments with different kinds of soundboards. The guitar with its hollow body to increase the sound was used in Egypt before the children of Israel made their famous passage through the Red Sea.

There were lutes, too, with still longer finger boards. These had graceful pear-shaped bodies and were hung from the shoulder with orna-

The Egyptians broadened the bow into a soundboard

mental cords or sashes. The long finger
boards of lutes and guitars show that man had
worked out another of his problems. He had
found that, in effect, a string may be instantly
shortened by pressing it against the finger
board.

There were lyres without a finger board, and
with a shallow box-like soundboard. These
lyres were the favorite instruments of the Greek
people.

*What did men
use for strings?*

The strings for these instruments were made
of tightly twisted silk, or of horsehair, or from
the intestines of goats or camels. Such membrane was very skillfully prepared. Man, in
his experimenting since the day of the hunter's
bow, had learned much about making strings.

Part of the fascinating mystery about music
is how men in widely separated lands made instruments which were so similar. Before
their earliest history, the Chinese, the Arabians,
and the Hindus all had guitar-like instruments.
The ancient Hebrews used a psaltery, a harp,
and a lyre. In the very beginning of the Bible

*The lute had a
finger-board*

The Lyre

story (Genesis IV:21) Jubal is named as "the father of all such as handle the harp and the organ." What kind of harps did Jubal's children handle? The Jewish people left no pictures or sculptures to answer this question.

Most of these ancient stringed instruments were Pickers. The early Scrapers were not important and they were not found everywhere as the Pickers were. Until the magic violin was made, the harp was the most important of all stringed instruments. It seems always to have been the most beloved. In Egypt harps were sometimes placed in the tombs of their owners. The children of Israel, when carried away as captives, refused to sound their precious harps in a strange land.

What stringed instrument was most common?

But nowhere has the harp been loved as in Ireland. The figure of a golden harp is woven into the Irish flag. Its strains are woven with threads of gold through the life and songs of the Irish people. There are legends which tell of the harp in Ireland long before St. Patrick set foot on her shores.

However, regardless of legend, the history of the Irish harp begins with the history of the Irish people. A set of laws made fifteen hundred years ago gives the harper the same rank as the cow-chief, who was an important person in early history. A law in this same ancient code lays a penalty upon one who borrows a harp or "tuning-wood" (harp key) and fails to return it. Evidently harp keys were more important in Ireland than borrowed umbrellas are today!

Were Irish harpers thought important?

Irish history is made beautiful with tales of its harps. The story of the famous harp of Brian Boru begins in 1014 when, legend relates, its owner, then the ruling monarch of Ireland, was slain in battle. His harp, as well as his jewels, was rescued by his son. It must have been greatly prized, for two hundred years later, so the story goes, it was sent as a pledge to Scotland to ransom a famous Irish bard. A song handed down from those times tells how eight years later the Scots refused to restore the harp even for "whole flocks of sheep." In the year 1307 the precious harp was taken to England where for two hundred years it was kept as a treasure in Westminster Abbey. King Henry VIII of England then restored it to the descendants of the first owner. After two hundred and fifty years more, during which time it changed hands many times and was robbed of its jewels and its silver trimmings, the famous harp was presented to Trinity College, Dublin. There it may now be seen as one of Ireland's most cherished antiques.

What is the most famous of Irish harps?

Ireland has other famous harps. Many stories tell of kings and queens who played them, of thieves who stole them, of knights who rescued them, of minstrels who sang with them, and of soldiers who carried them thousands of miles into distant lands.

Outside as well as inside of Ireland the harp has a history filled with romance and adventure. Wherever men have gone, they have taken the harp with them. They have improved it greatly since the days of the Irish bards. Of course, even in those times, the

The Irish harp is famed in both story and song

harp had already been given a front pillar to strengthen the frame. When this was done or by whom is not known. It already had the three-cornered shape when it was used by the ancient Greeks, and ever since then it has kept this form. The soundboard, or back, and the front pillar rise from the base in a V. At the top they are joined by the gracefully curved neck. The strings are stretched between the neck and the soundboard.

What great improvement was made in the harp?

The greatest improvement was made about one hundred and fifty years ago. A piano manufacturer in Paris invented a set of foot pedals by which the player can instantly shorten or lengthen the harp strings, thus making them sound a half step either higher or lower. These foot pedals are in the base. They move rods hidden in the front pillar. These rods in turn move little wheels hidden in the neck to which the strings are fastened. This is very complicated. Only a real genius could have worked it out. Because of his invention, the piano maker of Paris, Sebastian

Erard, (a-rahr) became the most famous harp maker of history.

The modern harp has forty-seven strings. The C strings are colored red, and the F strings are blue. This is to help the harpist as the black keys on the piano help the pianist.

Why are some harp strings colored?

For hundreds and hundreds of years the harp was the most important stringed instrument. Other Pickers came and went, but the harp remained. The Scrapers seem to have been little used.

About the time Columbus discovered America many changes were taking place in the world. Books were printed, colleges were founded, schools were opened. Music, too, was changing. More attention was paid to instrumental music. New kinds of songs were being made. The bard no longer furnished the only musical entertainment. Princes in their castles had orchestras and bands. The church had instruments to help the singers. Neighbors and friends met to sing, much as people today meet to play bridge. The practice of singing

The modern harp has a front pillar and pedals

soprano, alto, tenor, and bass parts together was the newest pastime. Everybody was "doing it." If an alto or bass were missing, that part was taken by an instrument. An instrument also helped choir singers learn their different parts.

What early instrument was played with a bow?

Here the Scrapers began to be important. A bowed or rubbed string produced a more singing and prolonged tone than could be made by picking. The stringed instrument of those days which was best suited to this use was called a rebec. It was something like the mandolin of today, but was played with a bow. The English called it a "fiddle." The Germans called it a word which meant "jig." Its tones were loud and harsh. An old Spanish poem speaks of the "squalling rebec." Such a voice was well enough for the use of street bands, and for fairs and village dances. Something better must be made for these new ways of using music in the church and in the home.

For many years the best stringed instruments of the world had been made in a small district

The "squalling" Rebec

of northern Italy. It was a land of new ideas, for in those years it was the meeting point of East and West. Travelers from distant places halted there. Merchants and sailors passed that way. Pilgrims and soldiers made it a stopping place. Bards and minstrels sang brave tales. There Italian painters mixed rich colors for their pictures, and there Italian sculptors gave to their marble the grace which was all about them.

It is not strange that the men of that region took the greatest of pride in their workmanship. The cabinet makers were expert craftsmen. The instrument makers were artists. They dreamed of bringing a wonderful new music from the strings. Yet they were doers as well as dreamers. They listened to the music brought by travelers from East and West. Ideas which might help were borrowed and passed from workman to workman for testing. Each was striving in friendly competition to make the instrument which would produce finer music than had ever yet been heard.

Why were the best instruments made in Italy?

These workmen believed that the strings with a hollow box for a soundboard held the secret of this unheard music. The best that had yet been made was the clumsy heavy-toned viol. But no workman was satisfied with it. They made viols of different sizes. They changed the shape of the body. They altered each different part.

How did the instrument makers improve the viol?

As they worked the voice of the viol took on a brighter sound. But yet it did not satisfy the workmen. Still they tried to make it better. They changed the curve of the sides. They altered the shape of the top. They arched the front or the back. They used different and thinner woods. They raised the bridge on which the strings rested.

Year after year they never tired of experimenting. The town of Cremona became famous because of its skillful workers. Patiently and happily they tested and tried each pattern.

At last a small, fine, clear-sounding viol was made. The master of the shop and his workmen gave the new viol an endearing name such as they would give to a beautiful child.   They called it the violin (little viol).

But there was one among the craftsmen, young Antonius Stradivarius (strah-dee-vah-rius), who still was unsatisfied.   When he drew the bow across the strings of the violin he still bent his ear above the delicate shell of the body, seeming to catch an echo of tones that had not yet been sounded.

Who was Stradivarius?

Year after year the boy worked on in the Cremona shop. He helped to make instruments of the violin family to replace the family of viols. His fingers grew more deft as he helped to make the tenor violin, which is the viola of today. His ears grew keener in the years he helped to perfect the violoncello, the bass of the violin family, as it is made today.

The years as they passed seemed to weave a spell for his working. He had a magic sense of touch. His fingers on wood told him just how it should be shaped. Each smallest one of the more than fifty pieces of the violin was

Year after year the makers experimented with violins

shaped according to its own character. His charmed fingers curved and molded soft wood for the front. They rounded and shaped the strong wood for the back. They joined front and back together with sides that fitted as exactly as the halves of a shell that have grown together. Every hidden slip of wood, every least peg, was perfectly made. The varnish, under his brush, welded them together into a violin which at last gave to Stradivarius the magic music of his dreams.

Has the secret of the perfect violin been told?

This is a true tale of magic, for the secret of the perfect Stradivarius violin was known only to its maker. The thin, shell-like little body, less than fourteen inches long and weighing less than nine ounces, is so perfectly balanced that it supports the pull of its four strings when they are stretched to a tension of sixty-eight pounds. No scale of measurement has been discovered by which instruments of such perfect proportions were constructed. The Stradivarius varnish also seems to have possessed magic, for never since has such a liquid been mixed.

Little is known of the life of Stradivarius. As a boy he was apprenticed to a violin master of Cremona.   His life story is told in the perfection of his instruments.   Other violins made by other Cremona craftsmen bring fabulous prices, but a violin bearing the signature "Antonius Stradivarius" is the almost priceless treasure of the music world.

Was Stradivarius the only great violin maker?

CHAPTER VI

FROM SONGS TO SYMBOLS

(How Music Was Written)

WHAT is the most famous ladder in history? It is a ladder which cannot be handled or touched, and yet a little child may move it up or down. It is used every day by old and young, rich and poor, by opera star, and by whistling newsboy. Yet it has never been seen.

What is the scale?

This is not a riddle. The name of this famous ladder is the scale. Its rounds or steps are the different tones used in making music. Each scale tone is a certain distance higher than the one just preceding it. Scale is another word for ladder. Every person who sings or hums or whistles or plays an instrument uses this invisible ladder, because every piece of music is made from a set of tones or scale.

92

There are different kinds of scales. The
do-re-mi kind with which every school boy is
familiar shows how scale tones are related to
each other.   No matter whether *do* is sounded
high or low, *re* is always the same distance above
it.   From the sound of *do, re, mi, fa, sol, la,* or *ti*
the pitch or sound of any of the other six in
the set may be found.   In this same way the
tones of every scale are related to each other.
Some scales of olden days had only five tones;
others had as many as twenty or twenty-four.
In the thousands and thousands and thousands of years man was learning to make music
he used certain tones over and over again.
These tones were the ones that his first good
horns and pipes had sounded.   When he was
learning to make the harp, he tuned the strings
so they would sound these same tones.   He
used them in the songs that he sang.   He made
scales to name the sounds used in music, but for
hundreds of years he could find no way to make
signs with which he could write what he sang.
This is why there will always be mystery

*Is there just
one scale?*

about the music of long ago.   Ancient people, before they had the alphabet, left sign writing which told *about* music.   They left pictures showing musical instruments.   But they left no signs or symbols to represent the scales they used, the melodies they sang, or the tunes they played.

Why have we no ancient music?

What lullaby did the daughter of Pharaoh sing to the baby Moses whom she found in the cradle of bullrushes?   When the boys of Egypt cut flutes from the reeds of the river Nile, what tunes did they play?   What was the work-song of the slaves as they heaved the stones of the great pyramids into place?   What melodies did David the shepherd boy use when he sang to King Saul?   To what music did the Greek girls toss their bright colored balls?   If the story of Emperor Nero fiddling while Rome burned is true, what tune made him so indifferent to what was happening?

The answers to these questions are hushed forever, because the people of those days had not discovered a way to write their music.

Boys cut reeds along the banks of the old Nile

The ancient Hebrews, Chinese, and Arabians wrote music in symbols. But these were interpreted only by their own trained musicians. There are stories which tell how the Greeks wrote music by using letters of the Greek alphabet as signs to sing by. They used other signs to represent tones sounded by their instruments. But although today the poems and stories of Greece are found in many school readers, nobody knows any of the tunes of the Greek people. After Rome conquered Greece all Grecian music was forgotten.

How did the Greeks write down their music?

In later days, about the time of the birth of Christ, the Romans also used letters of their alphabet as signs to show how a tune was to be sung. But these letters did not represent music exactly. No one could be certain how a tune written in alphabet letters was intended to sound. For hundreds of years men experimented trying to find how to make symbols needed to write invisible and constantly moving melodies. They found they must discover how to represent tones; how to show the relation of tones used in the same melody; how to show the time belonging to each tone of a melody, and how to represent pitch. They must discover some way of writing a tune so that everybody looking at the writing would be certain to sing it the same way.

What must written music show?

All this time, while the musicians were working, Rome was sending its armies into strange countries to conquer people who were still wild and uncivilized. Later when Roman civilization fell before the onslaught of the fierce tribes of the North, there followed a period of several centuries known as the "Dark Ages."

The only schools of the Dark Ages were the church schools or monasteries. Here, with the church, there might be a hospital, a shelter for the poor, and a lodging for travelers. There were kitchens where many could be fed. There were buildings where men and boys could learn a trade, and gardens where food was grown. These monasteries were built in many countries, even wild, uncivilized lands. They kept the light of learning brightly burning.

The monks in their monasteries were busy writing music for the churches

The work of the monastery was all done by
men called monks whose lives were given, without pay, to this work for church and people.
They cared for the sick of the whole countryside. They looked after the poor. They
worked the farm and garden. They did the
teaching, too. The monastery had very set
rules. Each monk had his own duties. From
morning prayers before dawn until bedtime he
worked busily.

At certain hours during the day all work was
laid aside. Everybody went into the church for
services, which the monks tried to make like
the service in the great church at Rome where
some of them had been trained. There the
singing was done by a splendid choir of men
and boys. This choir also chanted prayers and
responses. So out in these monasteries men
were taught to sing the church songs, to march
in stately processions, and to chant reverently.
Music was their recreation.

The monks found that music helped them
in many ways. One very good monk who was

*What people
were most
interested in
music?*

called the Venerable Bede said, "Music is the most worthy, courteous, pleasant, joyous, and lovely of all knowledge; it makes a man gentlemanly in his demeanor; . . . music encourages us to bear the heaviest afflictions, administers consolation in every difficulty, refreshes the broken spirit, removes headache, and cures crossness and melancholy." When music could do all this, no wonder the monks were willing to teach men to sing.

What was a cantor?

Usually the monastery had a singing master, or cantor. It was his duty to provide music for the services, train the men and boys of the choir, and make new songs for the service. All church music was made according to very set rules, and only the trained choir might sing. In the famous monastery of St. Gall in Switzerland the cantor found that the congregation also wanted to sing. He made hymns in which the untrained voices could join. These hymns were very popular, although one monk said the singing by the congregation was "like the noise of cart wheels rumbling over stones."

Each monastery had a singing master

*It was the cantor's duty to train the choir and to make new songs for
the services of the church*

Nevertheless, it attracted people to the church and helped them so greatly that even the Pope wanted to improve it. To this day visitors to St. Peter's Church at Rome may see, chained in its place, an old music book written by Pope Gregory nearly fourteen hundred years ago.

What did Gregory do for music?

Pope Gregory thought if the monks were to be the music teachers they needed more training. He started a school at Rome where the cantors or singing teachers for the monasteries were taught. They studied nine years. Only the leader could have a book. In those days printing had not been invented and all books had to be written by hand, and there was still no way of writing music so it could be easily read. The monks had to memorize all the songs. In the school at Rome and out in their monasteries some of the monks were able to compose music. They made beautiful new songs for the service. The monks tried to improve the written symbols for music in order that these new songs could be sent to other monasteries.

While they were experimenting, new kinds of music were being made. For many years all songs had been just melodies without tenor or bass parts. The monks began to add bass to the tunes they sang. At first it droned along on just one note as though some sleepy fellow had forgotten to go on from his first tone. But the choir liked the bass idea. Soon cantors were having to train their choirs to sing songs in which three and four melodies were going at the same time. This was called "discanting" or "singing apart." This new way of singing was probably more exciting than it was beautiful. But the choir practiced every day, and never went back to the old way of all singing the same tune.

What was "singing apart?"

Another change in the music began when organs were first used in the church service. Now the monks had to write music signs for the organist as well as for the singers.

Many of the cantors or monk teachers, whose names are forgotten, were very fine musicians. The name Guido (gweé-do) will be remem-

This song "Sumer is icumen in" was written by an English monk in 1240. The chorus reads "Sing cucu nu, Sing cucu, Sing cucu, Sing cucu nu"

bered as long as the *do-re-mi* is sung, for it was
he who gave these names to the scale tones.) It
happened in this way: Guido had his troubles.
It was not easy to teach the rough men of his
choir to sing new songs. Sometimes they did
not sing the old ones as well as the good monk
wished they would. A story of those days tells
that their singing sounded as though they were
"quarreling among themselves rather than
praising God." Of course the poor men had
no books and they probably did the best they
could to remember how the tunes should go.

*Why did
Guido want
names for
the notes?*

Guido kept trying to work out some way by
which to help them remember just how each
scale tone sounded. He was thinking about
this one day as he listened to the men sing the
Hymn to Saint John. The men knew this
song and sang it very well. Guido noticed
that each line of the hymn (except the last)
started on the tone of the scale next above the
tone with which the previous line began. There
were seven lines to the hymn. There were
seven tones to the scale. Here was a grand idea!

He would use the first syllable of each line as a name for the scale tone it sounded, except, of course, the last line. But he would give the syllable in the last line to the seventh tone regardless.

After that when the men could not get their tones right, Guido had them hum from the well-known hymn the line which began with the tone needed. Soon it was necessary for them to hum only the first syllable to get the correct tone, *do, re, mi, fa, sol, la or si,* as needed.

The hymn was sung in the Latin language. This is why the scale names are Latin. Here is the *Hymn to Saint John* which gave the scale tones their names: (*Ut* was afterwards changed to *Do. Si* is made up of *S* for Sancte and *I* for Ioannes—Saint John. It was later changed to *Ti.*)

Hymn to St. John the Baptist
V R 20897

These words mean:

> Grant thy servants may
> Sing in harmony.
> From evil free
> Thy servants' lips
> That they thy wonders
> May proclaim,
> Holy Saint John!

Guido's plan made it so much easier to teach a new song that it was used by other monks. The Pope heard about it, and sent for him to come to Rome and explain it. Legend tells how Guido taught the Pope a new song in one music lesson. The Pope was so delighted that he ordered all monks in all monasteries to use Guido's plan. From that day to this singing teachers have continued to use the *do, re, mi* method of instruction.

Why was Guido's plan useful?

Guido has been called the "Father of Music," because he worked out so many helps for both singers and teachers. It is said that he drew the staff lines to show the pitch of the tones.

About this time, instead of the Roman alphabet letters, the signs for tones were queer little black squares or diamond-shaped blocks

*Old and new forms of notes
and rests used in writing
music*

which later were called notes. A letter was placed on the staff to show the pitch or key of the scale tones. The clef signs of today grew out of these Roman letters. Clef is the French word for key.

What was still needed in writing music?

' All these new symbols and signs helped. Day after day and year after year the monks in their cells or tiny rooms of the monastery patiently copied by hand the songs for the church service. They found new signs and symbols to represent the new music of the day. They still had great trouble in teaching the choir how to sing in parts. The bass could not keep with the tenor. None of the singers could keep together. The music symbols for whole and half or quarter notes had not yet been invented. There was no way of showing a singer when to hold a tone or when to go on to the next one.

It was about one hundred years after Guido drew the staff that a monk named Franco made notes to show which tones were long and which ones were shorter. He made solid

The C, F and G clef signs used in the 13th, 15th, 17th, and 19th centuries

black notes and hollow white notes, some with stems and some without, quite as they are made today. He made rests to show when and how long a singer should be silent.

It was Franco, too, who placed a sign at the beginning of a piece of music to show whether the rhythm moved in three beats or in two. He called the three beats perfect, and used the symbol of a circle instead of the sign ¾, such as is used today. He called music with two beats imperfect. For this sign he broke the circle. Today Franco's broken circle is the mark for common or 4/4 time.

What were the first rhythm signs?

Now, when printed music is so common, these familiar symbols seem simple. They were not simple to those hard working monks. Monks lived hundreds of miles apart. There was no mail service, no telephone, no way of sending messages except by foot or horseback. Even roadways were few and very poor. The monks could not meet and talk things over, yet they had to work out symbols which they would all understand.

It took years to decide even the little matter of how to make the sign for a sharp. The sign for a flat was used first. It was the Roman letter b. The sharp was made by scratching over the sign for the flat. Finally only these scratches were used, and as years passed the scratches were made into the sign used today.

During all those hundreds of years the monks who made sacred songs to suit the church services and the minstrel bard who made story-songs to suit his listeners, were not the only song makers. The common people, or folk, also were making music. They made it to suit themselves and did not trouble about rules or about ways of writing it down. Their songs were made just for the fun of singing. Whenever people got together they had games and dances at home. They sang about themselves, and about their neighbors. They sang about love-making and about weddings; about planting and harvest. Many of these songs were quickly forgotten. Favorites were remembered and sung over and over.

What are folk songs?

People sang about themselves and their neighbors

Such songs are called folk songs because they were made by untrained singers and were easily learned and sung by the common folk in every land. The dance and game songs were full of the life and joy of the people. All were very different from the slow-moving, dignified hymns of the church. They were different, too, from the long ballads of the minstrels.

Some of these folk tunes were so pleasing that after a time they were borrowed by the monks and used in the church service. Of course the tunes used in this way must be made more dignified. The tenor voice would sing the rollicking folk tune while other voices moved along above and below the melody in a manner which gave a feeling of stateliness and reverence.

How did the monks use folk-tunes?

The monks were not the only admirers of the folk tunes. At village fairs and country festivals, or wherever crowds of people got together, a rebec or fiddle would strike up a dance tune and a jolly crowd would come together. The lilt and swing of the folk song

Not only the "folk", but those of high degree listened

were catching. Even the "lady of high degree" stopped to listen.

*Who were the
Troubadours?*

Perhaps this is why noble and knight who felt quite superior to the common people began to make songs for themselves. Such courtly singers were first called Troubadours (troó-ba-doors), from a French word meaning to find or invent, for they invented their own songs. In Germany they were called Minnesingers (min'-neh-sing-ers), which means singers of love songs. The strange part of the Troubadour story is that after the gentleman had made his song, he either could not or would not sing it himself. Instead he hired an assistant, or proxy, who could play the lute, to sing it for him, even when it was to be sung to the "lady of high degree."

The lady must have liked this sort of second-hand love-making, for in the course of time Troubadours entirely replaced the bards. These Troubadours followed the example of the minstrels in going from place to place with their singing, but they sang songs of romance.

*The Minnesingers were
singers of love songs*

From the age of the Troubadours comes the *serenade,* or evening song, sung under the window of a lady. The *nocturne,* or night song, and the *aubade,* or morning song, are also a heritage from Troubadour days. One of the most beautiful of all star songs, *Oh Thou Sublime Sweet Evening Star,* was written in the style of a Minnesinger by the great modern composer Wagner (vahg'-ner).

These noble singers vied with one another in making new kinds of songs. Contests were held, the prize for the best song being the favor of a fair lady. After a time many a Troubadour sang his own songs, and many learned to play their own instruments. Yet they kept their assistants, and often to the lute player and singer these knightly musicians added a juggler or clown. With such a company of entertainers the singer was sure of a welcome from everyone.

What were the early music contests?

Besides making songs which were different and beautiful, these "singers of chivalry," as they have been called, improved music in other important ways. Their songs were borrowed by the church and gave more grace to its staid formal music. They inspired the common people to make finer songs.

Who were the Meistersingers? The Meistersingers (mī′-ster-sing-ers) of Germany were shopkeepers and tradesmen who formed guilds or clubs to study music. Hans Sachs, a cobbler of Nürnberg, was a famous member of this German organization.

Although these songs differed from the dignified music of the church, they were made of the same invisible materials: rhythm, melody, and harmony. Strangely, too, all these old songs fitted into one or the other of three forms which are still used by song writers today. In music the *form* is as important to the composer as a *plan* is to a carpenter or a model to a maker of automobiles.

Song forms which have come down from these early singers are: the one-part song form in which one simple melody is repeated for each stanza of the text; the two-part in which there are two melodies, one of which is often used as a chorus or refrain; and the three-part in which the music for each stanza is made up of three simple melodies, or of two melodies the first of which is repeated after the second.

Who first represented music in writing?

While these different types and patterns of songs were being made and sung outside the churches, the monks in the monasteries were working out signs and symbols which would represent music in writing. At last, by the time printing presses began making books, music, too, was ready to be printed. In 1501 A. D. the first music book was printed. In 1 A. D. music had been represented by letters copied by hand; it had taken fifteen hundred years to make printed music! After all, this was not such a long time considering all that had to be done. In those fifteen hundred years man had made not only song symbols, but songs as well. The symbols and the patterns he had worked out were to be used for the songs of all the singers yet to come, the forms or patterns were to be followed by the makers of the world's greatest music.

CHAPTER VII

FROM NATIONAL TRAITS TO TUNES

(A NATION SINGS ITS OWN SONGS)

SUPPOSE some night as the town clock strikes twelve the covers of your song book should suddenly open, like the doors of a concert hall, and the songs appearing as people should step out from between the pages.

Who was Franz Schubert?

Suppose Franz Schubert, the world's greatest song maker, should act as director and announcer, and help you to give a song concert. He would probably begin with the oldest song. It makes a good opening number, for everyone could join in singing it.

The oldest song would come as a man because it is a man's song. He might wear the armor of a knight because almost one thousand years ago he rode with the Crusaders. He might look like an Arabian shiek, or an Egyptian

112

The Crusaders sang going into battle

camel driver, for he has been claimed by both. He might be dressed to represent the great composer Beethoven (bay'-toh-ven), who one hundred years ago borrowed this tune from the past to use in one of his compositions. He might even come in quiet modern dress—as an English lord, an Irish "paddy," a Rotary Club president, a high school boy, or anyone else who has sung a song to the tune of *We Won't Go Home Until Morning,* for this is the oldest tune in the book.

What is the oldest song?

Of course each of these singers would use different words. The English sing *For He's a Jolly Good Fellow.* The Irish sing *My Father and Mother Were Irish,* and a high school class takes the privilege of any words that are convenient. During the Crusades, with words of its very own, this song was sung in the Holy Land. There it was called *The Song of Mambron.* Everyone who heard it seems to have carried it to his homeland. This explains why the home of the little tune itself has never been traced. But for this special midnight concert the oldest tune appears in a track shirt singing *The Sophomores Own the High School.*

The very fact that the opening number was a song without a country suggests to Schubert the idea of calling for other songs by countries. Being German he naturally calls first for something from Germany, "the land of song and story."

In answer *A Mighty Fortress Is Our God* comes as Martin Luther, with all his inspiring personality. At the sound of his voice, as at the turn of a dial, into the room bursts a mighty chorus of Christian heroes. These voices sing the melody in unison as they sang it four hundred years ago in church, on battle-field, and at the martyrs' stake, but alto, tenor, and bass parts come surging in from the many who have sung it since.

Luther has much to tell. He explains why he favors hymns for the congregation to sing. He tells how important music has always been in the life of the German people; how in his day, four hundred years ago, and for hundreds of years after, each wealthy landowner of *The Fatherland* had his individual court, and maintained his own chapel and director of music. He tells how reverence for God, love of home, loyalty to country, and satisfaction in music are characteristics of the German people. As Luther returns to his place, Schubert explains that these qualities are expressed in the music of the German people.

He adds, "Characteristics of all countries are expressed in their songs." Then a happy little tune comes tripping from the pages of a book. It might have appeared as an Italian boy out of the past, or as the famous tenor Caruso, singing, as only he could sing, the most popular of all sunshine songs, the beautiful old Italian melody, *O Sole Mio*. But instead of either of these it is a child with a basket of grapes singing only *tra-la-la*. The little tune without words tells of blue skies, blue seas, fragrance of vineyards, beautiful gardens, and Italy.

As the Italian peasant song finishes, the an-

What is a favorite sunshine song of Italy?

nouncer speaks of the friendly happiness of Italian melodies which express the spirit found among Italian people whether working in fields or in cities. He tells how even the fishermen of the Bay of Naples sing songs which have the grace and charm of their sunny land.

How does the climate of Sweden affect her music?

Then with a smile he turns to "the land of the midnight sun" and asks for a song. *When I Was Seventeen* comes as Jenny Lind, the Swedish nightingale, in the bright holiday costume of a village girl. Like the little song, sometimes sad and sometimes gay, all Swedish music has its contrasts. Long dark winters seem always to add a strain of sadness to a Swedish song. One visitor to this country says, "Deep and dark and tender is the music of the Northland." But the game-songs and dances of the short bright Swedish summer are gay and jolly. Then the whole country bursts into sudden bloom. Everyone is joyful. Night is only a brief purple shadow. The people sing out their happiness for the sunshine. In Sweden, June 24th, the day that has

Italian songs express the spirit of the people

no night, is a legal holiday. The Midsummer Festival finds the homes decorated with birch boughs, and every village green bright with dancers. People seem to try to put a whole year of joy into their romping songs and games.

Jenny Lind gives place to a young man who represents the Norwegian love song *Last Night the Nightingale Woke Me*. As he finishes singing he points to a map of Norway saying, "See how the coast is cut by the dashing icy waters of the ocean. Here are the fjords which every Norseman loves. The wind sings its own weird music around the high rock-walls which rise above the clear water of these inlets. Back of these are the craggy mountains. From their caverns myths of trolls have given a touch of mystery to both the words and tunes of many Norwegian songs. Norway also has sunny meadows where the grazing herds and flocks help make the contented songs of summer days. The cold winters have developed sturdy songs. But the long dark days add a plaintive tone to much of Norway's music. The short bright

How does the Norway climate reflect itself in music?

Sometimes a whole year of joy is put into one Swedish romping song

summer gives a touch of gaiety that is sometimes almost boisterous. You must know that
the geography and climate of a land are reflected in its music."

*What is the
story of
Amaryllis?*

The announcer wants something very beautiful to follow this love song. With a formal
bow he asks to hear from La Belle France. The
narrow aisle broadens magically to make
room for a bridal party from the year 1581. A
princess, Margaret of Lorraine, on the arm of
the bridegroom, a grand duke of the day, leads.
Courtiers and ladies in brocade and cloth of
gold follow. The party dances the changing
figures to the familiar music of *Amaryllis,*
which was written for this very wedding four
hundred years ago.

Beautiful music! It comes from the land
where all workmanship must meet the test
question, "Is it beautiful as well as useful?"
From the Eiffel Tower down to the tiny por-
celain vase, and from the bolts of factory cloth
to the fine hand-made lace, everything must be
made to express beauty. Even the cakes of

*The Gavotte, a French dance,
    was brisk yet dignified*

Amaryllis was written for a bridal party in Lorraine more than four hundred years ago

France are made in attractive shapes and decorated in tempting colors. French artists have used the suggestion of music in making common labor beautiful. Jules Breton (bre-tōn') lets the peasant girl of his famous picture hear a lark-song, to lift her face and light it up with wonder. Millet (mē-yā') gives his weary toilers the *Angelus* (an'zhe-lus) to put reverence into their bowed heads and drooping shoulders. The charm of music and music of charm are important in the life of La Belle France.

How has music helped the Artists?

Before the last strain of *Amaryllis* has faded or the bells of the *Angelus* are hushed, without waiting for invitation out from between two leaves steps a jolly fellow. He gives himself a great shake crying, "Begorah! and it's glad I am to get out from thim book kivers! How should thim blessed young folks know about me?" And without more to-do he makes his way to the platform singing as only a son of the "auld sod" can:

> *Oh, Paddy dear, an' did ye hear*
> *The news that's goin' round?*

*"Wee folk of the
Emerald Isle"*

*What is the
music of
England like?*

As he reaches "The wearin' o' the green," the room is filled with "wee folk" of the Emerald Isle. They are perched about everywhere, strumming tiny harps and scattering Irish magic like moonshine all over the room.

As the music finishes, the last elf disappears. The announcer himself comes to with a start. "The land where laughter through every tear drop gleams," he repeats softly. And then he adds, "The Irish people have told their joys and their sorrows in their songs and have added their blarney and their fairies for good measure.

"How the songs do reflect the life of a nation. The music of Merrie England is like its healthy, happy, sturdy people. They have put their traditions into song." Just then, the sound of a hunter's horn rings through the room, and *John Peel* with his hounds is just appearing when a queer old man with a long white beard and long white hair and carrying a small harp steps before them. "Permit me," he says courteously, and without waiting for leave or license from Director Schubert he walks to the front of the room. With much feeling he sings the long ballad of *Barbara Allen*.

Just as he finishes a timid voice comes from the rear of the room. "Ye didn't get the ending the way we sing it up 'Troublesome'." A girl in a homespun dress with a sunbonnet over her face comes toward the old gentleman. The announcer smiles. "Will you tell us about your mountain ballads of America?" he asks so kindly that the barefoot girl pushes her sunbonnet back from her face and comes closer.

"I've been wanting to tell you all about us," she says. "You see, we songs came to America before there was any United States. We sailed with the first immigrant families that landed at the settlement of Jamestown. Other songs like us came with other shiploads of immigrants from Scotland and Ireland. By and by these immigrants adventured into the remote wilderness of the strange land. Cutting their way around and over mountains they came at length to grassy valleys and sheltered coves. Here

When did folk songs first come to America?

springs and streams offered water; trees furnished logs for cabins and wood for hearthfires.

"The men 'raised' log houses. The women laid home fires. There were soft moonlit evenings for 'followin' song,' there were broad hearth-glows for night-long 'story-singings.' There we old-time songs lingered and made new homes.

What important changes were taking place?

"Years and years later the settlements of the New World grew into cities. Printing presses and books came with schools that taught new songs and stories. The trails of the early immigrant had become overgrown with wild thyme and mountain laurel. But back in the mountains, in other valleys and coves, other cabins had been 'raised' and other hearthfires glowed, but always we folk songs made our place in the new homes. Always with banjo and fiddle we were handed down from sire to son; with reel and spinning wheel we were passed from mother to daughter.

"The favorite story-songs, or 'song ballats', as we are called by the mountain singers, are

The mountain trails were overgrown with laurel

the 'hurtin' kind'. The mountain folk sing
the Barbara Allen ending this way:

"Oh, father, oh, father, come dig my grave,
Dig it both deep and narrow.
For my sweet William died in grief,
And I will die in sorrow."

William was laid in the old church tomb,
His love in the churchyard nigher.
From William's grave grew a great red rose,
From Barbara's grew a briar.

They grew and grew to the old church top,
Till they could grow no higher.
And then they tied a lover's knot,
The rose wrapped 'round the briar.

The old gleeman takes the barefoot girl by
the hand. "Your old story-songs may be sung
now to the music of the banjo, but your ancestors
in Merrie England were sung to the strings of
a harp." Then he chuckles, "Let's sing *The
Frog He Would A-Wooing Go.*" The two of
them go down the aisle humming together the
"m—m, m—m" of the old English nonsense
ballad.

Franz Schubert looks after them, then he

*What is one
American
characteristic?*

says, "One American characteristic is to do old things in new ways. And while we are listening to the New World songs let us hear how the American Negroes made new folk songs from the music passed down from their ancestors of Africa." As he speaks, from a shadowy corner of the room there comes a soft humming sound like the tones of a pipe organ played during a prayer. Little by little the sound grows stronger as if coming nearer, but no singers appear. The humming sounds die away mysteriously and one voice alone, like a single organ melody, sings:

What is one of the best-known Negro spirituals?

"*Swing low, sweet chariot.*"

Out from the shadows comes an answering chorus of many voices—soprano, alto, tenor, and bass, all tuned together as the tones of a great organ are blended:

"*Coming for to carry me home.*"

The chorus dies out again in perfect rhythm. With just a little change of the first three tones, as if to make the melody more interesting, the solo voice repeats its first sentence. Again the full chorus responds, using its same words and changing only the last three tones to bring in a feeling of rest on the word *home.*

Then comes the solo voice with a new tune: "*I looked over Jordan, and what did I see?*" The chorus answers with its first tune. The solo voice again comes with the little change of tones:

"*A band of angels coming after me.*"
The chorus comes with sweeping tones as if all the pipes of the great organ answered. The song finishes as it began, with a soft humming of voices all perfectly blending together.

There is silence in the room and then the voice of Schubert asks, "Can you tell us how the Negro spirituals were made?"

From out of the shadow a voice with softened accents speaks. "Our ancestors in Africa, as all people of every tribe and nation have done, made songs to express their feelings. Our great-grandparents in the United States felt a great longing for a homeland of their own. The stories of the Bible heard in their camp meet-

What great longing does the Negro spiritual express?

Their harmony came from long association in cabin and field

ings gave them pictures of such a place. They
sang to express their longing. We sing these
songs as we remember hearing our fathers sing
them."

"But can you tell," Schubert asks, "how it
came about that the songs were made in such
perfect designs, as if some trained musician had
given a pattern which showed how the chorus
must answer and balance the solo voice?"

*Why can Negroes
sing part songs
without training?*

The voice replies, "All folk songs make a
pattern. To the verse tune some have a
chorus added, or a verse tune may have a contrasting part. So it is not strange that the
Negro also made his songs as all good songs
have been made. It is strange, though, that
while other races have had to be trained to sing
in parts, Negroes, without any training, sing in
natural harmony. This, we think, comes from
our long association in groups in the cotton
fields and cabins. The feeling for interesting
little rhythms we now believe was inherited
from our African ancestors, for men are finding
that the African Negro uses these same unusual

rhythms which our great-grandfathers sang into our spirituals."

Schubert smiles. "I see the time is fast slipping away," he says. "Will you sing for us once more, before we go back into our pages?"

The answer comes in a chorus:

> I got a song,
> You got a song,
> All God's children got a song.
> When I get to Heaven
> Gonna sing a new song,
> Gonna sing all over God's Heaven.
> Heaven, Heaven,
> Gonna sing all over God's Heaven.

The sound of a key turning in a lock! The song hums away into silence as the covers of the song book close like the doors of a concert hall when the people have all gone.

Chapter VIII

FROM BARDS TO BANDS

(How Orchestras are Different)

IN THE days of the spear, battle-ax, and long-bow a king might decree war, a chieftain might plan the attack, but a bard led the men into battle. He preceded the soldiers singing hero songs to stimulate their courage, and twirling and tossing his gleaming spear to entertain them. The drum major of today, with his twirling stick, is a descendant of this old-time leader. From the spear-tossing bard to the high school band is a long, long march. It is a procession of the music makers of the common people, for bands have always belonged to the street, the village green, and the public park.

What a movie such a procession will make produced in sound and color! The lights are

Who were the first drum majors?

128

Bards, gleemen, and skalds

dimmed. The curtains swing back. The early bards wander across the screen one by one, wrapped in long cloaks and chanting to softly sounding strings. Gleemen of old England and skalds who sang to the daring Vikings appear among them. Then minstrels, at first as lone wanderers but later in twos and threes and then in great companies, pass by. The first minstrels appear in the dull dress of the old bard. As the procession moves on, the cloaks shine with a luster of velvet and silk. They begin to gleam with gold and jewels which were gifts from royal hands. These minstrels in rich robes are seen to move in separate bands, each with its "King of Minstrels." One famous group passes in "gowns of cloth of gold furred with ermine."

Who were some of the old music-makers?

As the cloth of gold and ermine group passes, the procession begins to show here and there a clown or an acrobat or a juggler. The music also is changing. The old time hero song is replaced by folk songs. The harp is replaced by bagpipe and fiddle. Mingled with these in

Minstrels in cloth of gold

the procession is an occasional troubadour with his lute, or a minnesinger with his harp.   But mostly such singers would not belong in a procession of music for the common people.

Why were musicians not always welcome?

Little by little the marching bands become less and less impressive in appearance, but no less interesting in this march of time.   Groups of vagabond pipers and singers dancing and begging, juggling and stealing, as was convenient or expedient, pass across the screen.   They are pursued by bailiff or sheriff, for by this time being a member of a strolling band was about as respectable as being a gangster is to-day.   Even though musicians were not professional cutthroats, nor "people without-the-law," an occasional bad man really belongs in this procession.

But, although social outcasts, they were a merry company. Forbidden by law to play the trumpet and drums which were reserved for people of rank, they appropriated any tune they heard and sang it with words of their own making.   They poked fun at everything from the

Pipers, fiddlers and singers

church to the king, made and broke their own laws, were despised by all, yet were heard with delight by everyone. As the old-time bards had broadcast the news of the day, so these strolling musicians spread abroad the newest tunes. They were welcomed into the homes of the lowly and were furtively brought into the homes of the nobility, for they were the only teachers of the "popular" or people's songs and dances.

Among the fiddlers and singers in this long procession, occasionally appears a very important Town Piper heading the musicians of the town guild. At first such groups came only from large towns where tradesmen, who enjoyed making music, banded together to improve the art. They crowded out the vagabond musicians, declaring they degraded it. Now the music of the procession becomes more interesting, because with the passing of the years more and better instruments had been invented, and more and more town bands were organized. Little by little all communities of any size formed musicians' guilds or clubs.

What were the musicians' guilds?

Strolling bands of vagabond players

*Who was the
Piper-King?*

Strutting along very pompously in the procession every now and then comes the Piper-King. It was his duty to take care that no piper, drummer, fiddler, or player on any instrument be allowed to perform unless properly enrolled as a guild member. The musicians' union is not so modern after all! The Piper-King provided or arranged the music of all festivities. The number of musicians was regulated by the rank of the family giving the festival. A "full band" could only officiate on civic and state occasions, or in a religious festival. An alderman could employ only a certain number of the band players. If a citizen employed more than four to six pipers both the citizen and the Piper-King had to pay a fine.

These town bands of old have fifes, flutes, oboes, bagpipes, fiddles, viols, and drums. In the course of time the sound of horns and trombones is heard. The procession begins really to march in something like a band formation. Little by little the Piper-King had arranged for music in the church. Impressive bands of horn

*Musicians of the
town guild*

players, four to six in a group, pass, playing a simple old choral in beautiful harmony. These are the "town players," appointed to play chorals from the belfry of the town church on Christmas Eve, New Year's, and Easter.

By-and-by, above the dance tunes of strolling fiddles, and the sound of the viols and flutes of the town band, comes the ear-splitting din of trumpets. The early English word for band was "noise." The "Royal Noise" of the court of King Henry VIII (the English Bluebeard and musician King) was composed of fourteen trumpets, ten trombones, four drums, four tambourines, one bagpipe, three rebecs, and two viols! No wonder its name was "noise!" In those years each court had its trumpeter corps. The greater the court, the more trumpeters, and the larger the "noise." These were not bands for the common people, but when they marched the common people heard them.

What was the "Royal noise?"

As the court bands pass, the sound of marching feet changes to the sound of horses' hoofs. The cavalry bands come into view. Trumpets

King Henry's "Royal Noise"

do not make very interesting music unless the meaning of the trumpet calls is understood. Each different call had been taught by ear. It was a military band secret which could not be trusted to written notation.

What was the first regimental band?

As the cavalry passes a new kind of military band appears. It is the first official regimental band of France which King Louis XIV had organized under the leadership of Lully (lū-lē′), the greatest musician of his time. The music is different because Lully composed military marches to be played by flutes, oboes, and bassoons with drums. To be sure, French military bands with trumpets and horns follow in the procession, but these are quite separated from the reed bands. Whether trumpet or reed, these bands from the days of King Louis XIV were splendidly uniformed, for if Louis XIV liked anything better than music it was gorgeous finery and showy dress.

In watching and hearing such a procession it is fun to listen for the voice of the clarinet. It was a great day for band music when this in-

The mounted military band

strument was invented.   With the French horn to help, the procession of the music of the people now steadily improves.

The procession is brightened, too, by the brilliant uniforms of the state bands of different nations.   The Coldstream Guards of Scotland, the Prussian Life Guards, the Paris Guards of France, and a dozen others, each preceded by its national standard, pass in splendid review. Finally, among the passing standards, the flag of the United States of America appears.   Following it comes the famous Gilmore band represented as it toured Europe in 1878.   These marchers from our homeland are followed by splendid music from Old World organizations of tradesmen and laborers—factory hands of England in splendid bands, playing *Rule Britannia, The Hallelujah Chorus,* Mendelssohn's (men'-dels-son) *Wedding March.*   This is truly music for the masses made by their fellow workmen.

Suddenly from the echoes of the many horns comes a familiar strain.   John Philip Sousa and

What were other famous bands?

Splendidly uniformed musician-soldiers

his United States Marine Band playing *The Stars and Stripes Forever* brings every spectator to his feet. The most democratic of all band masters, the first American musician to receive an English decoration, is wearing the medal of the Victorian Order which was bestowed upon him by King Edward himself. The passing of John Philip Sousa, important as it was, would be only an incident in an endless procession which marches on as the curtains swing together and light again floods the auditorium, for as long as man makes music for the people there will be marching bands in splendid pageantry.

For what was Sousa noted?

There are splendid bands which do not march. These are orchestral bands which play orchestral music. The difference between orchestra and band lies in the importance given to the stringed instruments. Violins and cellos are not good marchers and cannot be included in a marching band. On the other hand, wind instruments are likely to become unpleasant when played in large numbers indoors. In the past a band was sometimes turned into an orchestra by letting the extra clarinets and trumpets stay at home and filling their places with violins and other members of the string family.

Experiments of this kind began to be made about the time colonists were coming to America. When accompaniments for operas came into demand it was found that an orchestra with a dozen violins furnished a better background for singers than a band with the same number of clarinets and cornets. Little by little during the next one hundred years the distinction between band and orchestra became more clear. A band was open air music for marching and parades. An orchestra was concert or stage music.

When is an orchestra better than a band?

Orchestras are less spectacular than bands, and until the radio opened the concert halls to everybody they were also less popular. Now, instead of belonging to the wealthy few, the finest orchestral concerts of the world are heard in the most lowly places. Since this has come about, people are comparing orchestral and

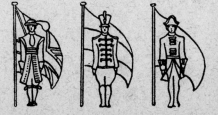

band music.   They are interested to learn why and how orchestral music is different from the music of a band.

What instrument made the orchestra possible?

The story of the orchestra began when the violin family replaced the viols, because up to that time what had been called orchestras were really only groups of players who accompanied singers.   Such groups were usually spoken of as bands.   The violin proved to musicians that instrumental music could be as expressive as vocal music.

When they found how to use the voice of the violin, they began to experiment with voices of other instruments.   They found that instruments, both alone and in combinations, could be made to represent different kinds and shades of feeling.

These were the days of great painters.   All people, the nobility and the masses, were interested in the masterpieces of their artists. Much attention was being paid to combinations of colors which expressed certain definite feelings.   People looked at pictures to find out how

The orchestra really began when the violins came in

the artist grouped his figures to bring about a balance that was satisfying. People understood that the arrangement of lights and shadows in a painting helped the artist to tell his picture-story without the use of words.

The makers of music gradually seemed to become aware that music, too, is a language which can speak without words. They began using instruments to express light and shadow, as an artist uses his color tubes. Also, as the artist arranges figures to give his pictures balance, so musicians began to use melodies to balance each other and make music that was satisfying. They worked out certain patterns or forms which became standard. All this took many years.

How do musicians use instruments and melodies?

Musicians experimented with combinations of instruments in connection with the operas which were then also an experiment in telling a story with music and words and actions. The instrumental players were grouped in a space between audience and stage. This space was called the orchestra. In Greek it means a place to dance. Musicians began to use that name for the instruments as a group. They spoke of music for the orchestra as they had been accustomed to speak of music for the church.

How were the instruments divided into groups?

In making orchestral music there was much experimenting. The most successful of the early composers was Haydn (high'dn). He tried using instruments as he might a group of singers. He treated the violin family as a choir. The violins he divided into altos and sopranos. The violas were his tenors and the violoncellos were the basses. For special bass effects Haydn used the big viols. Later on, the wood-winds made up another choir, the brasses still another, and all the percussions together made up a fourth group which became known as "the battery". Now with these four groups of instruments to combine, composers began to consider orchestral music as important as either opera or oratorio.

Listening to the experiments of musicians the public also began to discover the instrumental music, quite apart from either words or

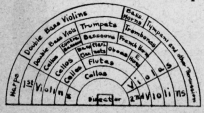

How the typical orchestra is arranged

acting, could be very interesting all by itself.
There were several reasons for this discovery.
All instruments were being improved. The
voice of the French horn was becoming soft
and beautiful. The flute tones were more true.
Valves were working wonders with all of the
wind instruments. The harp had been given
more strings. Its stronger frame permitted the
strings to be more tightly stretched. The piano
was developing. Best of all, the violin choir
was proving to be as expressive as a choir of
human voices.

*How were the
voices of the
instruments
made to sing?*

The second important reason why instrumental music of itself was found to be interesting was that schools of music had been estab-
lished, and men were learning how to combine
musical tones in groups called chords. They
worked out a science governing the use of
chords. Early builders made simple dwelling
places and knew nothing of the science of
architecture which later was needed in building
great cathedrals. Early artists scratched out-
lines of animals on rocks, but a masterpiece such

*Like architecture music developed
color, form and composition*

as the *Song of the Lark* could come only after centuries of experiments, which developed the science of color, form and composition.

The simple folk tunes had been the natural music of the people, made as the early shelters and pictures were, without thought of rules or science. The early monks, writing the church service, began the experiments out of which grew the science of harmony. Orchestral music developed as musicians learned more about the laws of this science.

How does the music of an orchestra differ from that of a band?

Since a marching band cannot use strings, its music is less varied than that made by an orchestra. The rhythm is very important. The tunes, the instruments, and the harmony all emphasize this primitive element or part of music, namely, rhythm. Everybody enjoys band music the first time he hears it. But people must have training to enjoy much orchestral music. They must have opportunity to hear it often. Learning to enjoy orchestral music without hearing it is like learning to swim without water.

Rhythm, tune, and harmony are equally important in orchestral music, but along with these the composer uses *color*. This is his name for the different voices of the instruments of the orchestra. The trumpet is described as having a *bright tone color*. The voice of each instrument has different shades of tone color. The trumpet tone can be made more brilliant or less bright at the will of the player. This is true of the voice of each instrument. A large orchestra has from eighty to one hundred players. Think of all the varying shades of tone color it can produce!

The composer of orchestral music must know how to mix and blend the tones of these instruments. He must depend upon players who are skillful enough to produce just the kind of tone he asks for and at just the instant it is needed in the music. There must be a very broadly trained interpreter, or director, who knows what effect the composer wants and how to help the players produce it. He is the conductor. For these men there must be days and weeks

What is "color" in music?

of practice alone and of rehearsal together. The men and the conductor are all experts and receive high salaries. This is why symphony orchestras can be maintained only in large cities.

Why is training in music appreciation necessary?

To enjoy orchestral music one must be trained to listen thoughtfully, to remember tunes, to recognize instrument voices, alone and in combinations, and to follow the design or plan upon which the composer builds his "cathedral of sound." School classes in music appreciation are training people to listen to music thoughtfully. Orchestras of the high school and radio are giving people opportunity to hear instruments played skillfully, alone and in combinations. In this way people are learning to listen, to enjoy the masterpieces of the orchestra, and to understand the language which speaks without words.

CHAPTER IX

FROM CHURCH TO THEATRE

(ORATORIO AND OPERA)

ORATORIO and opera are names for two different kinds of music-stories. They are not told or sung by one person as the old-time bard-stories were. Instead, for both oratorio and opera, the story is sung by a large group of people with a special solo singer to represent each leading character in the story. Oratorio and opera might be called musical twins, for both began in Italy in the year 1600 and in those days both were dramatized, or acted out, as well as sung.

Oratorio began in the church. The name comes from a church room where orisons (prayers) were offered. In those days such a room was called the oratory. The first music-story dramas were given in the church oratory.

What great forms of music began in 1600?

145

The other twin, opera, is named from a Latin word which means *operate* or *work* because the songs had been "worked" over beforehand and were not improvised, on the spur of the moment, as were many songs.

What do the names mean?

Since the year 1600, when oratorio and opera first appeared, they have been the two most talked-of kinds of music which man has made. For a time in Italy these twins grew up close together. Then their ways parted and each had its own history. Oratorio is the child of the church, and opera is the child of the theatre.

Fifty years before the first oratorio was produced the good Father Neri (nā´rē) in one of the churches of Rome was put in charge of the children and youth of the parish. He must have been as wise as he was good, for he understood that all work and no play was dull business. He arranged many of the lessons in the form of little plays or dramas, by which he could teach morals and religion. Then, knowing how the boys of Italy liked to sing, he chose the Pope's own chapelmaster to set parts of

the drama to music for boys' voices. At first there were only choruses in which all could join, but later there were solos for the best singers. They represented the characters in the story. But the chorus in which all could sing was the important part.

Another clever idea of the wise priest was to divide the musical play into two acts. The first act was used as a coaxer to bring the people to his service on time. Between the first and the last act the sermon was given. This was always a talk about the story which was being acted and sung. After this explanation the last act of the story was performed.

What did Neri do?

Father Neri knew that during two hundred years miracle and mystery plays, dramatizing Bible scenes, had developed into coarse and disgraceful performances. Because of this he took great care that the plays which he was sponsoring were both reverent and dignified. He dramatized *The Prodigal Son, The Good Samaritan,* and other stories from the Bible. He also dramatized stories from other sources as

lessons in moral training for the boys. To make these interesting he used both costumes and scenery. But he made the music more important than either of these. He seems never to have overlooked the fact that he was educating the young people who had been placed in his care.

Where did he get his stories?

For half a hundred years the plays which he arranged drew crowds to the chapel. People outside the church began to talk about them. They came to the notice of the poets and the musicians of Rome. Other persons besides Father Neri wrote verses for the chorus to sing. The finest musicians of Italy set the verses to music.

The first performance which was called an oratorio was given in the oratory of his church with very grand scenery and with gorgeous costumes, five years after the death of Father Neri. In many ways this oratorio was much like its twin, opera, and for many years in Italy, their early home, the chief difference was that oratorios always had a sacred story. Both had instrumental music, solos, choruses, and also a new kind of chant-like song for one voice alone. This was called a recitative because it recited the story which connected the other songs of the play.

While oratorios with costume and action were being given in the churches of Italy, musicians of Germany were setting to music the Bible story of the crucifixion, which was sung without costume or action.   Such compositions were known as *Passion Music*.   Passion oratorios, as they were developed in Germany, were far too sacred to be associated with any stage display.   The music itself could interest people and draw them to the church for worship.

What were the Passion oratorios?

The most famous of these passion oratorios were composed by John Sebastian Bach (bahk), who has made the world's most sublime and beautiful sacred music.   Bach had grown up a choir boy and his later life was spent as a singing teacher, and as organist and choir director.   His love of the strong, sincere choral of the Protestant church is reflected in his *Passion Music.* Bach's *Passion Music, Messiah,* and *Christmas Oratorio,* composed early in the 18th century, have been looked upon as the supreme works of their field, and they are regarded by musicians much as Shakspere's works are regarded by students of English literature.

Were all oratorios for church use?

In England at the same time another kind of oratorio was being sung. Bach had composed his *Passion Music* for church service. In England, Handel, another of the world's great musicians, composed oratorios for concert entertainments. Even though these were Bible stories, they were less serious than the *Passion Music* and were evidently written for amusement as well as for worship.

Handel was a German by birth. In his youth he, like Bach, had learned to sing the reverent hymns of the German church. When a young man he had traveled much. He had heard oratorios in Italy, where at that time more attention was given to letting the singer

show off his voice than to making the music express the meaning of the words.

Handel's oratorios were more showy than the *Passion Music* of Bach.   He used an orchestra which opened the story with an overture of instrumental music.   He used many different kinds of songs.   A solo for one voice alone, which Handel called an *aria,* might be a simple, sweet song with the voice singing above the soft tones of one instrument.   It might be a very dramatic song with many instruments to help emphasize the climax.   It might be a happy song where the voice made trills and turns as though imitating a canary bird.   Such a solo, if sung by a soprano voice, might have the flute to help express the feeling of grace and lightness of the aria.   Handel's *Largo* is an example of an aria.

What is an aria?

Handel used duets, or songs for two voices, which answered each other, one singing at a time or perhaps both together, making beautiful harmony.   He made trios, or songs for three voices, and quartets, or songs for four.

But Handel made the choruses the great feature of his oratorio. After three hundred years these are still the marvel of all who sing or hear a Handel oratorio. His masterpiece is the *Messiah.* The instrumental music is inspiring; the solos are marvelous; but when one hundred or more carefully trained men and women join in his great sacred chorus everyone feels like rising to his feet. This is what King George I of England did when he heard the *Hallelujah Chorus* from the *Messiah,* and to this day people follow his example whenever the *Hallelujah Chorus* is sung.

What are cantatas?

Since the time of Bach and Handel, many famous musicians have composed oratorios and cantatas (little oratorios). Easter and Christmas festivals are made beautiful with such music, and no longer are costumes or acting needed. Man has made sacred music which alone can draw people to the church service and hold their interest, because it has the power to express their deepest religious feelings.

While oratorio was growing and changing,

Handel made the chorus the great feature of the oratorio

the other twin, opera, had grown and changed, too. From the very beginning opera was planned for entertainment. While Father Neri in Rome was experimenting with Bible stories set to music and action, a group of Italian musicians and writers in the city of Florence, only a short distance away, were experimenting with old Greek stories set to music and action.

Who wrote the first operas?

It was only a few months after the first oratorio was given in Rome that the first opera was given in Florence. Its subject was a Greek myth. The opera was a part of the festivities for the marriage of the King of France to an Italian princess. It was a grand occasion. Visitors from many courts were present. During the festival the opera created more interest than the bride and groom.

After the festival the interest still continued. In those days Italy was the musical center of the world, and for the next two hundred years musicians from all over Europe came there to hear and study opera. An old-time announcement of the Italian opera described it as "an entertainment where intellect and all the noblest sentiments are fascinated at one and the same time by the most delectable art ever devised by human genius." The extravagant notice further pointed out that opera included literature, acting, singing in chorus and solo, instrumental music, dancing, costumes, and scenery. No wonder the world made a path to Italy to see what all the excitement was about!

What was added to opera?

The Italians and the musicians who came from other lands kept on with their experiments in this new kind of music. They tried different kinds of stories. They tried all the kinds of songs that were used in oratorio, adding dance songs and comic songs. Unlike the oratorio, the opera chorus was never so important as the solos, and for a time the whole opera seemed to be centered around the solo singers. Each character must have one or two very long and showy arias, no matter how they fitted into the story of the opera.

Although the chorus was neglected, the orchestra came in for its share of experimenting.

The opera chorus was not so important

Larger groups of instruments were used. These were improved greatly and the players improved, too. New combinations of instruments were tried out. Musicians never tired of working for new ways of making the orchestra help tell the opera story. One important musician of the city of Venice brought fame to himself by trying to represent in orchestral music the rippling of a brook, the roar of wind, and the murmur of the sea. What would he have thought if he could have heard the storm music of the *William Tell* opera! But that came two hundred years later, when instruments were still more improved and musicians had learned much more about combining them to produce certain effects.

How did the orchestra help opera?

In the first two hundred and fifty years of its life opera passed through many changes. During that time almost all of the great musicians composed operas. Each one had an opportunity to make his own operas better because of what the composer before him had done.

Finally came the man who is still known as

the "Master of Opera," the German composer, Wagner. He made changes and improvements of which no other opera composer had dreamed. He believed that music has power to express much more than actions or words. He believed that not enough attention had been paid to the opera story. He selected, from the literature of Germany, plots which could furnish him with strong characters and with very dramatic situations. Then he made a little tune to represent each character. As the various characters were associated in the plot he associated the tunes in his orchestral music. He did this so skillfully that his instrumental music told the opera story almost as plainly as the words and the actions of the characters. He was not satisfied that a singer have a good voice. He must also be a great actor.

Why is Wagner known as the Master of Opera?

These were only a few of the new ideas Wagner used in his opera. He proved his right to the title of "Master of Opera." But instead of opera, he called his compositions music dramas.

With the operas of Wagner and the oratorios of Bach and Handel the two Italian twins "came of age." The oratorio is the highest form of sacred music, and the opera is the highest form of dramatic music which man has yet made.

THE TRIUMPH OF THE ORATORIO

A STORY OF THE MESSIAH

About two hundred years ago there was deep distress in the Irish city of Dublin. There had been famine and people were hungry. There had been pestilence and people were ill. There had been war and people were injured. Worst of all, a law of the land permitted that any who were in debt could be thrown into jail. The prisons were filled, and charity organizations had no more funds.

Famine and pestilence in Ireland.

At this same time in England the great composer Handel was in deep distress. Through misunderstandings among his friends, jealousy among his singers, and rivalry among the composers of the time, his operas had failed. He found himself growing old, broken in health, and without funds. But his courage and his spirit did not falter. When a letter came to him from Dublin asking that he give

158

a benefit concert for the needy he gladly accepted the invitation. He agreed to write an entirely new oratorio for the concert. He knew that Dublin had plenty of people who would pay to hear his music, even though they were careless about helping the needy.

This invitation was a great stimulus to Handel. He forgot his own misfortunes. He decided to tell in songs the story of the coming of the Christ Child to earth. He could find no words better than the words of the Bible. He began with the Old Testament texts which promise the coming of a Messiah to comfort the distressed. As he worked he became inspired. Melodies fitted themselves to the sacred words in a way which led Handel to exclaim to a friend, "I did think I did see all Heaven before me, and the good God himself."

In a month's time the entire oratorio was finished. Handel called it *The Messiah*. The people of Dublin were much excited over the visit of the great Handel. They held high hopes of the results of his concert. An adver-

tisement in a "journal" of the times reads: "For the Relief of the Prisoners in the several Gaols, and of the Support of Mercer's Hospital in Stephen's Street, and of the Charitable Infirmary on the Inn's Quay, on Monday, the 12th April, will be performed at the Musick Hall in Fishamble Street, Mr. Handel's New Grand Oratoria, called the *Messiah,* in which the gentlemen of the Choirs of both Cathedrals will assist, with some Concertos on the organ by Mr. Handel."

The night before the performance there was a rehearsal of the oratorio to which those who had bought tickets were admitted. The crowd was so great that the morning of the performance the same journal printed the following notice: "The Stewards of the Charitable Musical Society request the favour of the ladies not to come with hoops this day to the Musick Hall in Fishamble Street. The gentlemen are requested to come without swords."

This was good advertising. By night everyone was talking about the concert. Because

hoop skirts and swords were not admitted, one hundred extra seats could be put into the hall and all were taken.

The concert was a grand musical success. A newspaper of the next day reported, "It took the people by storm."

Messiah scores huge success.

There were solo parts for leading soprano, alto, tenor, and bass singers. There were duets and quartets. But the great choruses were the grandest parts of the composition. Of all these the *Hallelujah Chorus* was the most wonderful. In it all the singers repeat this exclamation of praise over and over with every possible variation in accent and in melody. This leads up in a grand climax to the text: "For the Lord God Omnipotent reigneth: King of Kings and Lord of Lords!" It was of this chorus that a newspaper of the day reported, "It was allowed by the best judges to be the finest composition of musick ever heard."

The concert was also a grand success for the poor of Dublin. It furnished funds for their relief. It was also a great victory for the com-

poser Handel. The people of England heard
of the fame of his new oratorio. He was invited to give it in London where his last opera
had been so criticized.

King attends
London per-
formance of
Messiah.

The King and his court attended. This
alone would have made the occasion a social
success. But the King and the guests of the
royal party entirely forgot themselves in the
wonder of the music. They followed each
number with the greatest attention. When the
chorus burst forth with the first great Hallelujah, the King was so moved that he rose to
his feet. When the King stands no one remains
seated. On the second Hallelujah, as one man
the great audience arose, as to this day the
audience does whenever the *Hallelujah Chorus*
is sung.

Into the life of Handel *The Messiah* brought
beautiful harmony. The people who had mis-
understood him, the singers who had been
troubled by petty jealousies, the rivals who had
thought only of criticizing, united in praise of
the inspired music. It restored his broken

health and fortunes. It encouraged him to compose other sacred oratories. But of all his compositions *The Messiah* remains the masterpiece. Its music still thrills and inspires people as it did almost two hundred years ago.

Although Handel was born in Germany and became a naturalized citizen of England, he now belongs to every land where Christmas is kept. Each year his *Messiah* again tells in song the story of the coming of the Christ Child. It is a Christmas gift of music which never grows old.

Handel and Messiah belong to all the world.

CHAPTER X

FROM PAST TO PRESENT

(How Music Lives On and On)

WHEREVER a concert or opera is given, wherever people meet to sing or play music together, there among them though unseen are "shadow" musicians long since gone and forgotten. When a silver flute sounds, along with it from out the past a "shadow" shepherd pipes softly. When a player tests the tone of his horn, mysteriously as from some ancient forest a hunting call echoes faintly. The concertmeister draws a gleaming bow across the strings, and dimly, as if drifting on the smoke of faraway campfires, there comes a humming of taut bowstrings. Then, as the conductor lifts his baton, keen eyes may all but see the faces of musicians from the distant past who have made possible the music which the orchestra is about to play.

164

The fluting reeds, the echoing horns, and the singing strings are not all that the men of the past have given us of today. They have also given us the little tunes and the rhythm and melody patterns which have been borrowed and imitated throughout the centuries since man began to make music.

How does music grow?

Before Handel could compose *The Messiah,* there had to be men whose music he could study. These in turn had learned from music such as that sung by the choir boys of Father Neri. Still earlier were the folk who had made up miracle plays and acted them out with singing. Long, long before the miracle plays there were the great choirs of the Hebrew service in that fabulous temple of King Solomon which is described in the Bible.

Just as it is impossible to say of any time or place, "Here music began," so it is impossible to say of any composer that he created a certain kind of music. This is because every composer makes use of music-tools and materials which have been passed down to him by earlier mak-

Back of every violinist is the bow

ers of music. Nevertheless, a few great names suggest certain kinds of music.

Master of the Oratorio

GEORGE FREDERICK HANDEL

What a movie the life of Handel would make! Across the screen would flash one grand scene after another. For Handel became the friend of kings and nobles. He traveled from court to court and was everywhere welcomed with royal favor.

Imagine a few of the scenes from such a movie! The first shows the home of father Handel, who is a barber-surgeon in the German town of Halle (hah'-luh). The time is around the year 1688. Little George Frederick is toddling about among admiring relatives. He blows his toy whistle and trumpet joyously and beats his drum so rhythmically that mother Handel says he is surely going to make a musician. At this father Handel hastily

*The boy Handel stole away to the attic at night
to play on a clavichord*

gathers whistle, drum, and toy trumpet and
tosses them out the window. He will have
no musicians in his family! George Frederick is to be a lawyer. There must be no more
music in the home and the boy must never
go where music will be heard!

The second scene finds George Frederick at
the age of seven. In his night clothes he is
tiptoeing to the dimly lighted attic where the
clavichord has been hidden. The tinkling
sound of clavichord music brings a close-up of
a famous painting, *The Boy Handel.* This
shows the lad, nightcap upon his head, surprised by his family during one of his secret
practice-hours.

How did Handel get his start in music?

The next scene shows father Handel pre-
paring to visit a duke whose palace is forty
miles away. Amid the bustle of getting bags
into the carriage young George appears, begging to be taken along. But there will be
music in the palace of the duke. The boy
cannot go there! The carriage rolls through
the countryside. Suddenly father Handel dis-

covers his small son panting after it. The
carriage stops. The boy is severely scolded,
but—happy day!—he is taken along.

Across the silver screen now flashes room
after room of the palace, with George Frederick wandering through them at will. Soon
he discovers the object of his search, a fine
clavichord. Lovely music is now heard. The
charmed duke and the frantic father follow
the sound and discover the young player. The
father is shocked. The duke is entranced. To
the boy he gives a handful of coins, and to the
father some advice. He says, "Your son is a
musical genius. You must see that he is given
lessons."

Ten years have passed. During these years
Handel has studied busily. He has learned to
play violin, organ, and clavichord, and to compose music. He has even been the director of
a cathedral choir. Now he is in Hamburg
studying opera, the newest form of music.
Upon the movie screen appears the orchestra
of the opera company. The men are tuning

*To the boy a handful
of coins*

up for a performance. Among the violinists we see Handel. He is having fun pretending that he cannot play his part. But all the time his eye is on the harpsichord, whose player is absent. The director is annoyed. Where can the harpsichord player be?

Quietly Handel slips into his vacant seat. His hands run over the keys. Music fills the hall. The orchestra sits spellbound. The director stands amazed. Then as Handel pauses, the players of the orchestra rise to their feet to do him honor. The director begs him to continue.

How did Handel begin his rise to fame?

Now follow scenes in which the director is seen helping Handel with his first opera. At last comes the night of its performance. It proves a great success. Crowds of elegantly dressed ladies and gentlemen applaud wildly. Orchestra and singers crowd about the happy young composer. Music students clamor for lessons. Publishers request new compositions and, most exciting of all, visiting royalty from Italy invite Handel to come to that country.

Italy! In the year 1706 Italy is the art center of the whole world!

Films showing Handel's life in Italy would be very costly to produce. There would be splendid palaces where Handel played for crowned heads; cathedrals for which he composed sacred music for grand occasions; and concert halls where people thronged to hear the compositions of "the dear Saxon", as the Italian people affectionately called Handel. But in between these scenes of grandeur Handel would also be shown alone in his rooms, busily studying the music of Italian composers. For first of all he was in Italy to learn.

In what country did Handel do his greatest work?

After the Italian scenes there would come impressive pictures of Handel as director of music in the greatest court of Germany. But amid all the pomp and splendor, Handel would be shown looking longingly toward London. For his fame had already reached England, and he had been invited to write an opera for the Queen's Theatre.

To England he went and was so kindly received that he fell in love with the people and the country and became a naturalized Englishman. Movies of his English life would need to show the stage where his operas surprised and amazed his audiences. There would be showy music for these scenes to match the extravagant costumes and settings. For Handel never spared expense in staging his operas. Once he wanted to show a tropical garden; and to make it seem realistic he had dozens of live birds flying about the stage while, to an accompaniment of flutes, his heroine sang brilliant flute-like music.

The life of Handel could furnish all the variety needed for a good movie. He was the friend of the poor and humble as well as of the wealthy and powerful. One scene might picture him beside the anvil of a smithy from whom, it is told, he borrowed the tune for his famous composition *The Harmonious Blacksmith*. Another might show him spending the evening in the home of a coal carrier with whom he often spent a musical hour.

George Frederick Handel

There would be a touching scene when, through misunderstandings among his friends, jealousy among the singers of his opera company, and rivalry among the composers of the day, Handel faced failure. Under the strain, his health broke. His friends said, "Poor old Handel!" His rivals said, "Well, he is finished!"

How did Handel gain new fame?
But then there would quickly follow another scene showing how his courage and his genius met the crisis. He had composed cantatas and oratorios for church service. Now he would compose them for the theatre! He would amaze the people with his music instead of with stage effects. Instead of magnificent scenery he would provide magnificent choruses. He would replace showy costumes with brilliant solos.

At first the people were not sure they would like a sacred story sung in a theatre. They thought they must have costumes and staging to help tell a music story. But Handel knew how to win the public. He composed instru-

mental music to be played before the singers
began the story. He called such music a *concerto* (kohn-cher'toe). With concertos he
charmed the public into expecting fine entertainment. Then he never disappointed them.
He composed magnificent choruses to tell the
story of the oratorio. Between the choruses
he set solos, duets, and trios, which kept the
audience breathless, wondering "what next?"

Handel was always a swift worker. In thirteen years he composed thirteen oratorios. The
finest was *The Messiah*.

In the midst of new triumphs there came
tragedy, for Handel lost his eyesight. A scene
which made London weep would show the
blind old man, still erect and proud, being
led to the organ, where he played from memory or by inspiration.

But his strength was failing. A closing scene
for Handel's life-movie would show a great
funeral procession following his body to its
last resting place in the Poet's Corner of Westminster Abbey. In the procession would be

*How were his
last days spent?*

the great men of the time and the choirs of the
Royal Chapel and of St. Paul's Cathedral. It
would show England paying the highest honor
in its power to the adopted son who had given
the world its most-loved oratorio music.

Father of German Music

John Sebastian Bach

If the life story of John Sebastian Bach were
told in a radio serial, it would keep people
tuning in day after day to find out what happened next and to hear the music.

The announcer would say that the serial begins when Sebastian as a ten-year-old orphan
goes with his brother Jacob to live in the home
of their older brother, Christoph.

Sebastian took music lessons from Christoph, who was the organist in the village
church. But Christoph was a stern man and
paid more attention to the rules he taught
than to the genius of his small brother.

*John
Sebastian
Bach*

The first installment of the serial would have a background of beautiful music, against which the narrator would read.

. . . . . .

It is evening in the home of Christoph Bach. At one side of the hearth the wife sits knitting. At the opposite side Jacob and Sebastian study their catechism by the flickering light of the fire. At the clavichord Christoph is playing from a book of manuscript music.

Did Bach have a happy childhood?

Sebastian leaves the fireplace and stands behind Christoph. As the music comes to a close he steps forward eagerly.

Sebastian (*speaking eagerly*): That is beautiful, Christoph! I like that one best of all.

Christoph (*turning sharply*): To your catechism, Sebastian. You should be studying it, not listening to the music.

Sebastian (*eagerly*): I will learn my lesson tomorrow, Christoph, but now please may I play that music myself?

Christoph (*impatiently*): You? No, no.

You are too young. Go back to your
lesson.

Sebastian (*hopefully*): Then tomorrow?
May I take the book and play it for
myself tomorrow?

Christoph (*amazed*): What! Take my
precious book which cost me months of
copying! You know it is always locked
behind the grating in the bookcase.
You must never so much as touch this
book!

Frau Bach (*speaking kindly*): Come, little
Sebastian. Come, Jacob. We will now
sing the evening prayer, for it is your
bedtime.

(*Voices are heard singing an old hymn.
This fades away and the voice of the narrator
begins again.*)

It is midnight. Moonlight coming in
through the window shows Jacob asleep, while
at a table near by Sebastian is busily drawing
a music staff in his copy book. Jacob, roused
by the scratching pen, starts up.

Sebastian (*quickly*): Hush! Make no sound!

Jacob (*whispering*): What are you about, brother?

Sebastian (*whispering*): I must have the music! I can pull the book through the grating and copy the notes by the moonlight. Please, Jacob, make me no trouble!

Jacob (*sleepily*): Well, if you must be so silly, that can do no harm.

Sebastian (*softly*): Make no sound. I shall be back in bed when the moon is gone.

So night after night for six long months little Sebastian worked at copying the tiny black notes which meant so much to him. By day, in the absence of Christoph, he dared play the music he had copied. Then one unhappy day—

(*Background of music*)

Christoph (*coming into the room*): What is this? You have taken my precious book?

Sebastian (*proudly*): No, Christoph, it is

How did Sebastian obtain his copy of the music book?

my book. See, I have made a copy!
Listen how well I play the music!

Christoph (*angrily*): You disobeyed me!
You deserve to be punished. You stole
this music. I shall burn the copy!
(*Sound of rustling paper and heavy
steps*).

Sebastian (*begging*): No, Christoph! No,
oh no! (*The fire crackles. A door
slams. Sebastian sobs; and then the
voice of the narrator against the background of a Bach Choral softly played.*)

The copy was gone but in the memory of the
boy the melodies lingered on, to come alive
again in music which made John Sebastian
Bach the greatest musical composer of Germany, perhaps of all the world!

. . . .

The next installment would tell of the choir
school where John Sebastian earned his board
and room by singing, and where he had books
of music and an organ on which he might
play as much as he wished. It would surely tell

of the thirty-mile tramps which John Sebastian used to take to hear a famous organist. There is one special story of the night when, trudging back to school supperless and hungry, he stopped outside an inn to sniff the cooking food. Suddenly, out of the window came two herring heads. They were not a tasty tidbit, but better, thought the boy, than hunger. They proved much better, indeed; for when John Sebastian opened them, each head contained a coin. With one coin, he bought his supper. The other coin he saved for a later trip.

What good fortune came to him?

Organ music would play an important part in the installment telling of the day when Bach was invited to test the new organ in a near-by town. He was young and inexperienced, but he knew organs. First he played the instrument as loudly as he could to prove, as he explained to the committee, that it had good lungs. Then he played as softly as possible to prove that the lungs could be controlled. Finally, when he had tested every part, he

Out of the window came two herrings heads

played the music of the service so beautifully that then and there, although he was only eighteen years old, the committee offered him the position of church organist.

How did Bach fare as a church organist?

In those times the church organist was expected to compose music for the service. This the young organist was ready to do. He made beautiful hymns, which the congregation loved to sing because they were like old folk tunes. In some of them he really used old tunes, but he added to this music of the past his own beautiful touch and so created stately chorals which are still favorites today.

One installment of this part of the radio story of Bach's life would be a romance, for there is an old account of how the church committee reproved the young organist for paying too much attention to his young cousin Marie, a singer in the church. In those days such a reproof was serious business. But the romance ended happily when Bach was offered a better position in a near-by town, married his cousin, and lived happily. Within the next ten years

As the young organist played

Bach composed some of the world's greatest organ music.

Perhaps the next installment of the serial would be a story from his years as music conductor in the court of a wealthy German prince. The music for this installment would show Bach using folk tunes in a different way. The prince played a flute and was especially interested in intrumental music. In those days instrumental music, excepting organ music in churches, was rarely heard. To show that clavichord music could be interesting, Bach composed sets of different kinds of dances. First he would have a short prelude or introduction; then would follow in turn a stately old procession, a sprightly gavotte, a dainty minuet, and—for the close—probably a jig, which would make the prince think of a village fair or a carnival scene. Often for such sets of short pieces, which Bach called *suites* (sweets), he used tunes which he had heard in his childhood or perhaps remembered from some visit to a fair. But whether he used

What kind of music did he compose?

The committee listened

old tunes or created new ones in the style of the old folk dances, Bach always gave them a charm which delighted the people of the court.

Bach was always finding new ways of making music interesting. He decided that the different parts of his suites might sound better if played in different keys. But this could not be done on the clavichord because of the way in which it was tuned. With great patience and skill Bach worked out an entirely new plan of tuning the instrument. His plan was so successful that it has been called the "greatest invention in music history" and is still used in tuning all pianos.

In what ways did he improve clavichord music?

Bach's suites required quick finger action, but at that time clavichord players used only the three middle fingers. Imagine a three-fingered pianist today! Bach boldly taught the use of the thumb and the little finger. In this way also he gave greater charm to the instrumental music of all keyboard instruments.

For this German prince he composed music for violin or flute combined with other stringed instruments. These quartets and concertos, as Bach called them, are still frequently heard on concert programs.

In the radio serial there should also be a story of Bach as music teacher and composer for his family as well as for his prince. The music for this would be little *Preludes* which he wrote for his children. Children today still practice Bach's *Preludes* in their lessons.

In the midst of this happy music there would come the tragic story of the death of his wife, Maria, while Bach was absent with the prince.

One of the happiest installments of the Bach story would tell of his home life after he became director of music in one of the finest schools of Germany. After the death of Maria, Bach had married a young singer. She helped him with the music education of his motherless children. Now, in the new home in Leipzig with her own young children added, she helped him make their family musicals famous. In all, Bach had twenty children,

Was the Bach home a musical one?

everyone of them, as he wrote to a friend, "born musicians." Although the oldest were gone before the youngest were born, the Bach household was always large. Yet there were always extra violins and flutes and even clavichords for chance guests. The students of the school liked to drop in of an evening. With father Bach directing, what music they would make! Such an installment of the radio story would have to be a concert!

Bach must have been a tireless worker. It was while he was director of this school that the greatest of his choral music was written. His students supplied music for four churches, besides music for special events such as large weddings, important funerals, and great civic occasions. All this music Bach must compose and copy. Yet, it was here, for use at Easter and Christmas, that Bach composed the greatest music ever written for church service.

It is not strange that with so much copying of music, Bach should lose his eyesight. Like Handel, his last years were spent in total blind-

ness. But in other ways the lives of Bach and Handel were totally different. At his death, Bach was known to but few people even in his own country. Much of his music had never been published. For many years it lay unnoticed and dusty in the old school at Leipzig. Then, nearly a century later, another musician, Felix Mendelssohn, found the manuscripts of the great master and made them known to the world. Bach has been called the "master of masters" because of his influence upon later composers, including Beethoven and Wagner.

Was Bach always as well known as he is today?

The last installment of a Bach radio serial might come from the present. It could tell of the famous Bach festival which is held each year at Bethlehem, Pennsylvania. It might include people from all parts of the United States, who come together to hear as well as to sing and to play the compositions of this quiet, unassuming man who took the best from all that had gone before, gave it new value, and passed it on for all the music makers of the future to possess and to enjoy.

Father of the Orchestra
FRANZ JOSEPH HAYDN

The story of Franz Joseph Haydn (high'dn) begins in the kitchen of a thatched cottage in the old Austrian town of Rohrau (rohr'-ow), where he was born in the year 1732. It is evening. Before the fire the father sits playing his harp and singing old folk songs learned from his grandparents. The mother, busy about her kitchen, sings along with him. A clear, sweet childish voice joins in. The parents smile and nod towards the bench in the corner. There sits little Franz Joseph gaily fiddling with two pieces of wood. He is keeping time with his head and his stick-bow, for all the world like the village schoolmaster!

Did Haydn enjoy a happy childhood?

The director from the choir school, seeing Franz Joseph fiddle and hearing him sing, took him in as a pupil and choir boy. In such boarding schools the choir boys had regular studies and, in addition, special music studies. Soon Franz Joseph was learning to play a real

violin as well as the harpsichord. Then by accident he learned to play the drum. This is how it happened.

During a festival week the choir marched in a procession every day. But the drummer was unable to march. There was only Franz Joseph to fill in. He was too small to carry the big drum, but the director knew that he would keep the procession marching in time. He showed the boy how to hold the sticks and told him to work it out as best he could. Franz Joseph found an old tub and set to work.

How did Haydn make his first public appearance?

The procession that afternoon must have been very amusing! While a big boy carried the drum on his back, Franz Joseph followed close behind beating in fine style. The crowds in the street laughed, but they cheered louder than they laughed. The director was a hard man, but he too laughed.

For years Franz Joseph was soloist in the choir. He was a good student, but he loved fun and was often caught in mischief. As he grew older and his voice began to break, the director was less inclined to overlook his pranks. One day Franz Joseph cut the pigtail off the wig of the boy sitting in front of him. For this he was turned out of school without a penny!

What misfortunes came to him?

Franz Joseph now tramped the countryside to find work. By playing at festivals and funerals, he picked up a meager living. He slept in the attic of a poor musician who befriended him. The hardest trial was that he had no clavichord on which to try the music he was always making up. Sometimes he even had no paper to write down his tunes.

Once he wrote a serenade, and to find out how it would sound he coaxed two friends to go with him to try it out. They decided to sing it to the daughter of an actor. But when they sang under her window, it was the father who came to thank them.

"Who wrote that music?" he called.

"I did," boldly answered Haydn. The actor, who was just then busy writing a comic opera, took Haydn into the house and asked him to

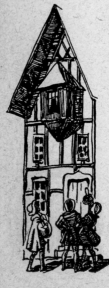

The serenade

compose some music for it. The plot called
for a storm, but Haydn could not make his
music loud enough to seem stormy. He lost
his temper and slammed his hands down on
the two ends of the keyboard, crying, "The
devil take the storm!"

"That's it!" shouted the actor. "Now you've
got it!" And he paid the hungry Haydn $55
for the music.

Haydn now rented an attic and an old
clavichord and even bought some paper and a
few books. The leaky attic seemed like heaven!

In those times there were two words which
musicians often used. *Cantata* meant a composition for voices. *Sonata* meant a composition for instruments. There were many cantatas but not so many sonatas, because the instruments of those days were not so good as
they now are. Haydn wanted to work out a
regular pattern for a sonata. He thought that
if musicians had no words to follow, they
would like to have the music make a design.
He knew that a good design would have to

*Franz
Joseph
Haydn*

have contrasts and different kinds of tunes arranged to make a pattern. He used some of

What did Haydn do to make sonatas more popular?

the old folk tunes he had learned from his father. He made up others that had the same happy lilt as the ones he had tried to play on his stick-fiddle. He worked very busily, and often forgot that he was hungry.

Now came better times. People began to listen to his sonatas. Musicians liked the way his tunes worked into a design. They liked the way he always made them follow his sonata pattern. Wealthy people hired him to compose music for their parties. Pupils came for lessons.

Then one happy day a nobleman of Austria engaged Haydn to direct the music for his grand country home. The castle stood in gardens which were like fairyland. It had concert halls, a theatre, a chapel with a fine choir and an orchestra with the best of players. What a change for Haydn! No more cold attics. No more tramping about to give lessons. And here were a choir and an orchestra to help him in working out his musical patterns.

The castle where Haydn first performed many of his symphonies

There was plenty of work. The prince had a concert every day. Haydn trained the choir and composed operas for the garden festivals. Often the prince invited a few friends into his private apartments for a quiet evening. It was for these little gatherings that Haydn made some of his loveliest music. He wrote quartets for two violins, a viola, and a 'cello. Today these string quartets are as fresh and charming as when they delighted the prince and his guests more than one hundred years ago.

In what other forms of music did Haydn achieve success?

But Haydn's best experiments were made with the orchestra. The men were so fond of jolly "Papa Haydn", as they called him, that they would willingly do whatever he suggested. He tried placing the instruments in different groupings, and formed a string choir which he seated in front of the other players. He found so many ways of improving the orchestra that he is called the "father of the modern orchestra". He composed sonatas for the orchestra. These were called *symphonies*.

All this time Haydn must be having his fun.

*How did his love
of fun show
itself in music?*

One day he came to orchestra rehearsal with his pockets full of toy instruments. To the players in their dignified lace ruffs and powdered wigs he passed out tin whistles, cuckoo imitators, toy trumpets, toy drums and rattles. Then he gave them the music for a new composition called the *Toy Symphony*.

At first they thought the master was only joking, but upon playing the toy instruments to the accompaniment of the music, they found that he had produced a really delightful symphony. When they performed it before the prince, he also was greatly pleased with Haydn's new composition. The *Toy Symphony* has been played hundreds of times since and still makes people smile as the prince smiled long ago.

Guests of the prince carried stories of Haydn and his music to other lands. Haydn was invited to visit England. While there he was given the greatest honors a musician could receive. But even while being entertained by nobles and princes, he had to have his fun.

He composed a *Surprise Symphony*. According to his regular pattern, the slow part opens with gentle music, but all of a sudden there comes a crashing chord which makes everybody jump! But the grand people who had come to the concert liked being surprised, and "Papa Haydn" became more popular than ever.

"Life is a charming affair," Haydn once said to a friend. He said the same thing many times over in his music. After all these years he is still saying it. For Haydn left the world a matchless gift of charming, happy music.

Master of the Symphony
LUDWIG VAN BEETHOVEN

The story of Ludwig Van Beethoven (lootvig vahn bay'toh-ven) is the story of a gallant battle. It is the story of a matchless knight doomed to live in disguise and all his life to do daily battle with invisible foes. For his defense he had an invisible shield and sword.

Ludwig
Van
Beethoven

All this sounds as strange as an old-time fairy tale. But this story is true. The invisible foes were troubles more difficult to conquer than any dragon of fairy lore. The disguise and the invisible shield and sword—but these are a part of the strange story!

The battle began when Ludwig was only a baby in the German town of Bonn, where he was born in the year 1770. The father was a stern, hard man, a musician in the court band. Much of his small salary went for drink. The mother was kind and gentle, but she had little with which to make a baby comfortable. It was a poor home.

Why was Ludwig's childhood an unhappy one?

Ludwig was only four years of age when his father began teaching him to play the piano. "I will make a fortune by training the child to play in public for money," the father thought. Drink made him a severe teacher. Sometimes the lessons were given after he came staggering home from a tavern. He would pull Ludwig out of bed to sit for hours at the piano. A mistake meant a whipping. The child's tears and the mother's entreaties were of no avail.

Now the battle was really on. But for the struggle the little knight did have an invisible shield. It was the comforting care of his mother. This helped him against treatment too harsh for a child. He did have an invisible sword. It was his great love for music. This helped him with lessons too difficult for one of his years.

What shield of comfort did he carry?

Ludwig learned rapidly. By the time he was eleven years old, three of his compositions had been published. His skill in playing the piano amazed all who heard him. But for some reason little or no money came from his public concerts.

But new troubles began to make life difficult. The harsh treatment from his father and the long hours of study were affecting Ludwig's disposition. At school he was moody, and he kept to himself. He made no friends and never played with the other boys. But in this struggle the shining shield was again his help. An old organist, who had been a friend of grand-father Beethoven, found what a difficult time the boy was having. He helped him with his studies and taught him to play the organ.

But conditions at home were growing worse. His mother was ill. Ludwig must help support the family. At the age of thirteen he left school to earn what he could by playing in the court orchestra. He kept at his studies and by the time he was fifteen he was organist of the court chapel. Every spare moment was spent busily composing. Some of the music he wrote was published. But Ludwig was always wishing that he might have lessons in composition. He dreamed of going to the city of Vienna where he might study with great teachers and hear great music.

Why did he wish to go to Vienna?

Then one happy day the dream came true. Some friend, perhaps it was the old organist, made it possible for Ludwig to go to Vienna. He set off with high hopes and was soon at work with new teachers. Now it seemed that the shield of friendship was to help him win his battle. But the trouble-dragons were close behind him. He was called back by the illness of his mother. He reached home just as she was dying, but in time to promise her that he would take care of the younger children.

Now came hard years. He had loved his mother greatly. His grief for her, and the care of the home and children were almost more than he could bear. Instead of study and improvement, he must now be playing wherever he could and teaching in between times. There was little time for composing.

But these were not all the troubles he had to battle. Part of them were inside his own mind. He grew irritable and more moody. He was unhappy and frequently fell into despair. Then a kind woman, the mother of two of his pupils, began to take the place of his beloved mother. She saw what a difficult time he was having. She made him feel welcome in her beautiful home and, seeing that Beethoven lacked proper schooling, she arranged for him to share the studies of her

Who helped and encouraged the young musician?

own son. Best of all, she understood him in his moody and irritable spells. "These," she said, "are his troubles pressing upon him. We shall see what friendship can do for the boy."

Once more the shield of loving care helped in the battle! His devotion to music again became a gleaming sword. He studied and composed. His playing began to attract the attention of influential people. Life became less difficult. There were happy hours.

At last his brothers were able to care for themselves. His poor, weak father died. Soon a wealthy nobleman offered Beethoven a home in the city of Vienna.

In Vienna at this time music was very popular. People of wealth held concerts in their grand homes. Noblemen and ladies had their favorite musicians, who were discussed just as movie stars are talked of today. With the help of friends Beethoven made his way among them. He became the favorite musician of the city. He also began to gain renown as a fine composer.

Other composers made music which was interesting and charming. Beethoven made music which brought tears to the eyes. He made of music a language which told of joy or of sorrow, of despair or of gaiety.

How did Beethoven's music differ from that of other composers?

But a great sadness was with him in all his successes. He was very self-conscious. He had a knightly spirit and matchless genius, but his appearance was anything but knightly.

His manners, too, were "ugly." The strangest part of Beethoven's story is the way in which he treated his good friends and the way in which they cared for him. He would fly into a rage and call them names, forbid them to speak to him and abuse them spitefully. But the next day he would suffer remorse because of what he had done. His friends always overlooked his fits of temper. They felt that any person who could compose and play such music should be forgiven for rude actions. Thus even in his great success, his shield of friendship and his gleaming sword of music were all that kept Beethoven from despair.

He was often moody and sad

*What great
tragedy came to
Beethoven in the
midst of his
success?*

But the greatest dragon of all was near. Beethoven began to lose his hearing. In a letter to a friend he tells of his distress. "I pass my life wretchedly," he wrote. "For two years I have avoided all society because I cannot possibly say to people, 'I am deaf.' If I were in any other profession it would not be so bad, but for a musician it is a frightful position."

But he did not give up. He wrote some of the world's greatest music when he could no longer hear a sound. Always his friends stood by. They held a shining shield of care between him and this great new distress.

But now still other troubles were upon him. His brothers, for whom he had sacrificed so much, began to meddle in his affairs. They borrowed money, found fault, and even sold to publishers some compositions which Ludwig did not want published. A nephew whom he had adopted and whom he loved as in his boyhood he had loved his mother, caused him only sorrow.

At last his health began to fail. He could no longer take the long tramps in the fields which he had loved. But up to the end of his life his knightly spirit did not fail. In his last symphony he composed his great *HYMN OF JOY*. Music such as Beethoven left to the world could never have come from one who lost a battle. He lives on victoriously in music known and loved throughout the world.

Master of the Music Drama
RICHARD WAGNER

The story of Richard Wagner (vahg'-ner) begins in a theatre. His stepfather was an actor and often took Richard with him to rehearsals. The two were great pals, and after the rehearsal they would talk together about the theatre and about the different characters. Before Richard was eight years old, he knew as much about the great plays of Shakespeare as children today know about the movies.

Richard Wagner

When Richard was old enough for school, his favorite studies were history and literature.

Why did Wagner begin the study of music?

He liked to read stories of old Greek heroes and old German legends. He used to write plays of his own. Then he began to wish that he could write music to go with his plays. He decided to study music. Whatever Richard did, he did with all his might. When he took up the study of music, a friend said of him that he "ate and slept" with the music of Beethoven, that he went about the street "humming" the tunes of the Beethoven Symphonies.

He did so well with his music study that while still only a young man he was composing operas. But there were long hard years ahead. In those days it was not easy for an unknown composer to find a publisher for his works or a producer who would present them. Yet Wagner never gave up. For years, while trying his luck in different cities, he did all sorts of musical odd jobs to eke out a poor living. All this time he kept on studying and composing.

He was about twenty-six years of age when
on a long sea voyage his ship ran into stormy
weather. During four long weeks on board
the floundering vessel Wagner often heard the
sailors speak about the old story of the Flying
Dutchman. This old German myth tells of a
sea captain doomed to sail the ocean year after
year in a fearful ship with blood-red sails and
a ghostly crew. On and on the poor captain
must sail. Only once in seven years can his
ship make harbor. His only chance to break
the evil spell must come during his few short
hours on land. If he can find a girl who will
love and trust him, he will become free from
the curse.

*What gave
Wagner the idea
for "The Flying
Dutchman"?*

As Wagner listened to the talk of the sailors,
he thought to himself, "What a wonderful play
that old story would make!" As he listened
to the roar of the wind and to the rush of the
waves, he thought, "If only I could make
music to match that old story!"

The four stormy weeks at sea were not
wasted. The memory of them lingered and

The Flying Dutchman

often brought the story of the Flying Dutchman to his mind. Finally Wagner put the
story of the ill-fated captain into a poem and
the poem into an opera. Into the opera also
went some new music ideas. Wagner gave
each of the principal characters in the story
a special little tune or musical theme. Whenever in the opera the Flying Dutchman was
to appear, his theme would be heard in the
orchestra. But Wagner also made a special
theme or tune to represent an idea. For example, there was music to represent the idea
that the love and trust of a girl would redeem
the captain.

*What new ideas
did Wagner bring
to opera?*

In the orchestra music of the *Flying Dutchman,* Wagner used these special themes much
as characters are used on a stage. In the
Overture, which is played before the Opera,
the themes without the help of any words gave
a preview of what the Opera was to show.
The Flying Dutchman was a new kind of
opera. It was really a drama in which the
music themes were as important as the actors.

As he worked on the poem and the music and the staging of the *Flying Dutchman,* other old German legends and myths which he had read as a boy came to his mind. What music dramas they would make! But the old stories were filled with magic. They had talking dragons, magic swords, magic fire, and beauteous mermaids living in the depth of the great Rhine river. How could such characters be shown? How could such scenery be arranged?

Where did Wagner get the plots for his music dramas?

Such difficulties only made Wagner more eager to put them into his dramas. With the aid of music he could tell any story. Where a magic scene could not be shown, he would make magic music to express the idea. He retold the old folk tales in dramatic poems. He made dramatic music to match.

But this was a new kind of music. Even though Wagner was dramatizing their own old stories, the German people could not understand this new kind of music. Managers of opera companies would not present his operas. A few of the musicians of the time understood. They encouraged Wagner and helped him stage his music dramas.

At last the German people, too, began to understand. They began to talk about Wagner and his new kind of opera. Some liked it and others did not. But everybody liked to talk about it. This was good publicity and crowds flocked to every performance. At last success rewarded Wagner's perseverance.

How was his great dream realized?

But this was not enough. Wagner loved to dream dreams and make them come true. He had dreamed of a special opera house where even the scene of the mermaids could be shown. Of course in movies of today this could be managed. But in those times such a scene had to be left pretty much to the imagination. Now Wagner set about making his dream come true.

This was a great adventure. People in all parts of Europe and even of America subscribed money to help. Wagner himself made the plans and selected the little town of Bayreuth (bi'roit) for the location of the theatre. In its building every detail of Wagner's dream was made real. He had come to believe that costumes and scenery were almost as important as music and actors. When at last the building was completed, Wagner had all that his imagination could ask for.

There was a great festival. People from all parts of the world came to look and listen— and to worship. For the theatre became a shrine to which music lovers journeyed as on a pilgrimage.

Thus the story of Richard Wagner closes as it began, in a theatre. But the beginning was a small boy looking on at a rehearsal. The close was a great artist seeing his own drama, hearing his own music, and watching his own dreams come true.

In the story of "How Man Made Music" Handel, Bach, Haydn, Beethoven, and Wagner are great familiar names. But along with these is an innumerable company of all those who through the ages have helped in the development of this Divine Art called Music.

CHAPTER XI

FROM FOLK SONG TO SYMPHONY

(THE UNITED STATES MAKES ITS MUSIC)

MUSIC has been called "the universal language". It crosses boundaries and spreads over land and sea as freely as the air on which it is borne. It belongs to anyone who can enjoy it, no matter how or where it was made. Unlike other languages, it needs no translation.

This is why the music sung, played, and enjoyed in the United States is not greatly different from the music of the Old World. We love the great symphonies, oratorios, and operas of the European masters only a little less than do the people among whom they were composed. And the music which we create quickly spreads to the far corners of the globe and eventually becomes the possession of music-lovers everywhere.

Folk-tunes from Germany

An interesting story might be told about the growth of music in the United States from the coming of the first white men right down to the latest "folk-song symphony". To be sure, there had been music in the New World before the white men brought it—the music of the red men. Every Indian tribe and community had its own ceremonial songs and dances, many of which had been handed down from father to son for several centuries.

Who were the first music-makers of the New World?

To the invaders from across the sea this music had no meaning. As the tribes of the red men were broken up and scattered, most of their music became lost and forgotten. Only within the last fifty years have the people of the United States been interested in Indian music. It is now fully recognized as a part of American culture.

The story of United States music would therefore begin with the planting of the first English colonies. The early settlers of this country brought with them the folk songs and church music of their homelands. For many

Buffalo dance of the Sioux

years this was the only music known to them. The long, hard task of establishing homes and conquering the wilderness left little time or energy for the creation of new music. But with every shipload of English, Scotch, Irish, Dutch, German, and Swedish immigrants more tunes came from "the old Country".

From Old Erin

At first these various national groups kept to themselves. But as the country became more settled, the people and their tunes began to mingle. Immigrant customs, stories, and songs were exchanged. Pioneers learned additional melodies to sing at their spinning, their planting, and their occasional gatherings. Music was helping to conquer the wilderness.

Slowly the New World pioneers began to make a music of their own. But for many years much of this new music was made by recombining Old World melodies and supplying them with new words. The oldest national tune of the United States—*Yankee Doodle*—originated in this way. According to legend, it was pieced together by an officer of the

"Yankee Doodle keep it up"

British army quartered in the colonies during the French and Indian wars. Taking a snatch from an English folk air, a refrain from a Dutch harvest song, and a strain of a vintage dance from Spain or Italy, he supplied a foolish ditty designed to poke fun at the oddly dressed colonial soldiers. The tune became immediately popular, and a few years later was the favorite marching air of the rebel armies in the War for Independence.

How did "Yankee Doodle" come to be?

Many of the Old World melodies traveled with the pioneers into the backwoods country of the Appalachian Mountains. Here, of a spring evening, when the air was sweet with dogwood and honeysuckle, there would be a neighborhood "singin." Along the footpath to some cabin door would come men in buckskins with their "women-folk" in homespun. In the moonlight they would sing old story songs, or "ballats", which had been passed down to them by their Scotch or English ancestors. *Barbara Allen* was a favorite. New verses were added to it from time to time, until

Along the footpath to some cabin door

at last *Barbara Allen* was sung in almost as many different versions as there were communities to sing it.

How did music spread across our continent?

An exciting chapter of the story of United States music would tell how the immigrant tunes traveled on with the western trail blazers. Songs helped open up the Mississippi Valley to settlement. Songs went with the Mormon push-carts across the plains and through the mountain passes. Songs rode in Conestoga wagons into the Oregon Territory. Songs kept the "forty-niners" going in the California gold rush. One of the favorite songs of the day, sung to the tune of *Oh Susannah,* was:

> *Oh, Californy!*
> > *That's the land for me!*
> *I'm bound for Sacramento*
> > *With the washbowl on my knee.*

On all these difficult trails, tunes were sturdy travelers. In wilderness camp or lonely cabin they made many a happy evening. Perhaps there was a fiddle in the outfit. At the first

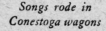

Songs rode in Conestoga wagons

strains of a jolly reel, "all hands" gathered around the firelit circle. Cares were cast aside. Danger skulked in near-by shadows, trouble waited down the trail, but for a merry hour the hard road was forgotten. If the fiddler ran out of old tunes, he made up new ones in the style of the old. It was in such places that *Arkansaw Traveler* and *Turkey in the Straw* had their beginning.

All this time in the eastern sections of the country more and more attention was being given to music. Singing schools improved the church chorus, some music was being printed in America, and the manufacture of instruments had begun. Many homes had little reed organs or melodeons, and bands were being formed in the growing towns. For serious study musicians still went to Europe, and the New World could boast no composer of note.

Then out of Pennsylvania came the songs of Stephen Foster, with a smile or a tear for everybody. *Old Black Joe, Oh Susannah,* and *Old Kentucky Home* took the land by storm.

What signs of progress appeared?

Many homes had organs or melodeons

One of the greatest song travelers of all time is Foster's *Old Folks at Home*. In the year 1852 a newspaper complained "that it was on everybody's tongue!" Then the homey little song became a globe-trotter, and in the last ninety years it has been sung from the arctics to the tropics and been translated into nearly every known language.

Why did Foster's songs gain so much popularity?

Foster's songs are as simple as folk tunes. Everyone can sing them. This is one reason for their popularity. They came at a time when the people of the United States were feeling the need of music that could be easily sung and played.

Another reason for their popularity was that everyone had a keen interest in the South and its Negroes. The minstrel show with its blackface comedians was the favorite amusement of the people in all parts of the United States. Many of Foster's best songs were first popularized by "end men".

The most remarkable songs of the United States are those of the southern plantation

Music of the Negroes

Negroes. This part of the story of United States music might begin in the jungles of Africa. It should tell of the ancestors of the Negro slaves, of their expert drumming on tribal drums, and of the ways in which they used bone and wood clappers to mark exciting rhythms for the tribal dances. It should tell of dramatic story-songs which a leader sang in short sentences, waiting at the end of each sentence for the whole tribe to praise his story in a short, answering chorus.

What is the story of Negro music?

The Negroes on Southern cotton plantations made up beautiful spirituals using this same pattern of sentence and answer. They had no drums, but in these new songs their voices kept the feel of the drumbeats and the exciting rhythms of the clappers. No story could explain how these untrained musicians learned to sing in parts. They made up songs in which soprano, alto, bass, and tenor voices fit together as naturally as the petals of a flower. This natural blending of melodies is the miracle of Negro spirituals, which many people regard as the rarest music yet to come from the new world. Several fine examples are included in the last chapter of this book, among them: *I Ain't Gwine Study War No More*, *Steal Away*, and *Swing Low, Sweet Chariot*.

What kind of music grew up on the western plains?

Another variety of folk music grew up on the western plains. In a wild West movie when the bucking broncho dashes onto the screen and its rider neatly ropes his "critter", nobody thinks of the cowboy as a singer. But in the old days every outfit had its songs, which the cowboys made to their own liking. Sometimes they borrowed a tune and adapted it to new words. One song which every cowboy knew was:

> Oh, bury me not on the lone prairie,
> Where the wild coyotes will howl o'er me.
> In a narrow grave just six by three;
> Oh, bury me not on the lone prairie.

These doleful lines are set to the tune of an old English song of the sea. Such songs were favorites with the men who rode the wide

Songs from the land of the wooden shoe

Cowboy songs about the chuck wagon

ranges with never a fence or a cabin for land-
mark.

(*Home on the Range* is one of the best-loved
of these cowboy ballads. The cowboys made
up both the tune and the words.) Other cowboy songs are *The Chisholm Trail, Poor Lone-
some Cowboy,* and *The Lone Star Trail.*

Some songs were made in relays! One cowboy would work out a chorus as he rode behind his herd, and at night he would sing it
to the rest of the boys gathered about the
chuck wagon. The listeners would get the
feel of the pony-gait in the tune and the breath
of the range in the words. One of them might
make up a verse to go with the chorus. Later
these would be passed on to other outfits, for
cowboy songs also were travelers. Through
months and even years the song would make
the circle of round-ups and rodeos. It might
even come back to the one who had started it
with a whole new set of words. The tune
might even be changed a bit, for cowpuncher
songs were passed by memory from outfit to

*How did the
cowboys make
their songs?*

outfit many years before ever they were printed in books or sung over the radio.

While the cowboys were "ridin' range" by day and singing their songs by night, people living in the eastern half of the United States were finding more and more time for cultural occupations, such as making and enjoying music. The larger cities built concert halls where visiting musicians played to large audiences. Operatic and symphony concerts came more into demand as the taste for music grew.

What did Mason do for American music?

Popular interest in music was greatly stimulated by the efforts of one man—Lowell Mason. He grew up in the years when the schools taught only "readin' an' ritin' an' 'rithmetic." Later he came to believe that boys and girls should learn to sing as well as to spell. He spent his time and fortune in proving that music deserved a place in the public schools of the United States. Thus he earned for himself the title, "The Father of Public-School Music."

Mason also composed several beautiful and

The square dance

simple church hymns which everybody could sing. *Nearer My God To Thee* is one for which he will long be remembered.

In cities such as Boston, New York, and even as far west as Chicago, notable symphony orchestras were soon organized. Series of concerts were given regularly, and the "opera season" in these cities drew music-lovers from all the surrounding territory. In the schools bands, orchestras, and glee-clubs were formed. Towns large and small had their marching bands.

These bands should have a chapter in a story of American music, and John Philip Sousa should be the hero of this chapter. With many a stirring composition he earned the title of "March King." When his big band circled the globe, he played before both royalty and the common people. His clean, crisp music made his audiences think of the United States as a happy place in which to live. He was the first American to receive an English decoration.

Foster, Mason, and Sousa are not what crit-

Who was the "March King"?

"Band concert night" in the early nineteen hundreds

ics would call great musicians. Yet each in a special way made music for the people. Each helped the nation along the road from colonial Yankee Doodle days toward the time when all kinds of people in the United States could hear and enjoy the best in music.

Many other musicians of the United States made music that all the people love. The Irish-American, Victor Herbert, with his melodious tunes set everyone to humming and whistling. He is best known for his operettas. *Babes in Toyland* and *Mlle Modiste* are two of the most popular. A favorite melody is the "Italian Street Song" from *Naughty Marietta?*

Perhaps the greatest musician the New World has yet produced was Edward Mac-Dowell. After years of study in Europe he returned to his New England home and translated its "wild rose" and "deserted farms" into music-language which everybody could understand. His whimsical *Woodland Sketches* proves the proverb that it takes a great artist to do a simple thing and do it well.

MacDowell was one of the first composers to use Indian themes in instrumental music. In 1896 his *Indian Suite* was played in New York City by the Boston Symphony Orchestra. This composition marked the beginning of interest in the music of the red men. Later composers have drawn freely upon Indian themes in their compositions.

In the field of popular dance music, America in recent years has led the world. It was in the early nineties that ragtime "cakewalked" its way into the musical limelight. Out of minstrel show days had come many a "coon song" with syncopated time. To these and the ragtime of the Negro dance there was soon to be added the weird harmonies and still stranger rhythms which have come to be known as jazz. Out of jazz has come the thing called "swing".

For what kind of music is America best known?

As in every other kind of music there are different qualities of jazz. Much of it is more noisy than clever. Such music is soon forgotten. But some jazz music will be remembered because it has real character and musical interest. The *Rhapsody in Blue,* a concerto for piano and orchestra by the American, George Gershwin, is the most pretentious jazz composition yet produced. It deserves a real place in the story of New World music. Jazz is considered by some people to be one of the two greatest contributions America has thus far made to music. The other is the Negro spiritual.

How did Damrosch help spread the love of good music?

What Lowell Mason did to help public school pupils learn to sing good music, three other musicians of the United States have done to help people hear and understand instrumental music. In New York City the director of the symphony orchestra, Dr. Walter Damrosch, believed that school pupils should hear orchestral music and should have opportunity to know the many different instruments by sight and sound.

He arranged for children's concerts to be given on Saturday mornings. For these he assembled his full orchestra and had it play a carefully selected program of instrumental

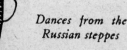

Dances from the Russian steppes

music which every one should know.   Before
each number was played, Dr. Damrosch explained how the music was made and what
part the different instruments would play. He
called men forward to show and sound special
instruments.   No wonder the concert hall was
crowded!   In those days this was almost the
only chance the average child had to learn
about orchestral music.

About the same time Theodore Thomas of
the Chicago Symphony Orchestra was giving
what he called "Popular Concerts" at specially
low admission prices. Through these he
reached, with his fine group of players, thousands of people who otherwise could not hear
such music. In connection with these concerts
Mr. Thomas said, "Popular music, after all, is
only familiar music," and he proved it by making the best music of the world so familiar that
men whistled it as they went about their daily
work.

While Dr. Damrosch was wishing he could
reach the children outside of New York, and

*Peasant music
of France*

*What has the
phonograph
done for music?*

while Theodore Thomas was touring the Middle West with his orchestra, a wonderful invention was being perfected. The phonograph was sufficiently improved that the music of great orchestras could be faithfully reproduced. By the time this was done a woman had already begun to make the dreams of Dr. Damrosch and of Theodore Thomas come true.

When first the phonograph began to reproduce good music, Frances Elliott Clark, a music supervisor in the public schools of Milwaukee, brought phonograph records into her classrooms. With these she helped her pupils to hear and understand music which before then she had been able only to tell them about. Her experiment was so successful that soon other teachers followed her example.

This was a new field. One of the large phonograph companies offered training for teachers who in turn should train others to carry recorded music into every school. They secured Dr. Clark to direct the undertaking. School teachers and pupils were enthusiastic

*Quaint rhythms from
the Orient*

about this new way of studying music. Within
ten years in remote country schools from Maine
to Texas, children became familiar with the
music which Dr. Damrosch could give only to
the children of New York City, and which
Theodore Thomas had given to the people of
Chicago. How Lowell Mason would have
loved it all!

Then came the radio! Through his famous
Music Hour, Dr. Damrosch, with his own
charm of voice and manner, could reach mil-
lions of school pupils every week. With special educational phonograph records prepared
under the direction of Dr. Clark, the radio lessons in music appreciation could be given previous study. In the most remote schools of our
land the world's best music is now being made
familiar.

During these same years music has come to
occupy a larger place in the schools. From the
rhythm bands of the lower grades all the way
up to the orchestral bands and choral groups
of high school, music forms an important part

*Gayer tunes from
Scotland*

of the student's program. In some parts of the country the schools furnish certain of the instruments.

In this chapter about school music two other important names deserve a place: Joseph Maddy and Interlochen. The first is the name of a man who had a dream, the second of a place where the dream became real.

For what will Joseph Maddy be long remembered?

While all this growing appreciation of music was leading to school bands and orchestras in every part of the country, Mr. Joseph Maddy, a public-school music educator, dreamed of a summer camp where high-school pupils might have weeks of training in hearing and making music. In the summer of 1926 he tramped through the underbrush and pine forests of northern Michigan to a place where two lovely lakes join waters. Interlochen! The name meant little then. Now it means a national music camp which each summer takes care of more than two hundred high-school students.

There are modern cottages for girls and their supervisors on one lake and for boys and their

*"My Old Kentucky Home"
is still standing near
Bardstown, Kentucky*

supervisors on the other lake. There is a great oak-shaded bowl seating eight thousand listeners. Here the campers give symphony concerts which are broadcast over nation-wide networks.

"Music in the air" might be the title for a beautiful story about America's out-of-door concerts and festivals. During the summer season in nearly every city and village, from the Hollywood Bowl to the Lewisohn Stadium in New York, people of every trade and profession gather in their own communities for an occasional evening of music. The music may be that of a noted symphony orchestra, as in the Grant Park concerts of Chicago or the Belle Isle concerts of Detroit. It may be a gathering of many music organizations, such as the annual Chicagoland festivals. Or the music may be made by the home-town band, as in countless small villages throughout the land. It may even be made by the people themselves, as in the festival held yearly on the field of Iowa's College of Agriculture. There every

What are some popular musical events?

Concert under the stars

mid-June a choir of one thousand 4-H Club girls and a chorus of eight hundred farm women make a choral background for colorful dances and pantomines. Members of their families gathered from all over the state make up the enthusiastic audience.

Do Americans like good music?

In all parts of America regular yearly festivals are held in which visiting instrumental and vocal artists join local orchestras and choruses in presenting operas and oratorios. The inspiration for such civic enterprises, the patience and courage necessary to carry on from year to year, the ever-increasing attendance, all bear witness to a growing love and appreciation for music on the part of the American people.

What will the future hold?

This widespread interest in fine music is beginning to call forth greater achievements than ever before in the creation of original music. Besides the light popular and semi-classical music for which American composers have heretofore been noted, more and more music of a serious classical nature is now being composed. After three hundred years of growing up, United States music is finally "coming of age." Its future is filled with promise. In the stirring words of the *Ballad for Americans*:

*"Our country's strong, our country's young,
And her greatest songs are still unsung!"*

Chapter XII

NOW WE SING

(Famous Songs Everyone Should Know)

THE making of a song is not an event, it is a process, for a song is made only in its singing.

The clever Japanese have discovered how to make pearls. They plant a grain of sand within the shell of a living oyster and wait for it to grow. With the passing of each day, year after year, the grain enlarges. Seven years the patient Japanese gives to the making of a perfect pearl.

Seven centuries may go into the making of a jewel of song. Year after year, with every singing a luster gathers about even a simple melody. A jewel of song adds to its worth with each new singing and shares its luster with each singer and with each new hearer.

The Star Spangled Banner

During the War of 1812, a young Baltimore lawyer named Key sailed down Chesapeake Bay to obtain the release of an American doctor held prisoner on board an English warship. Key reached the vessel just as the British began to bombard Fort McHenry. He, too, was detained as a prisoner.

All night from the deck he watched bursting shells and bombs as they exploded over the distant fort. In quick flashes of light he could see that the American flag was still floating. Toward morning the firing ceased. From his lookout Key could see nothing, and had no way of knowing which side had been victorious. Imagine his relief when the "dawn's early light" revealed the Stars and Stripes still floating.

In that hour Francis Scott Key wrote the first stanza of the song. Later in the same day, after his release, he wrote the other stanzas as he sailed back to Baltimore. Key fitted his poem to a rousing old English tune, already familiar to many people. The new song took the city of Baltimore by storm, and soon it was heard in every gathering of patriotic citizens.

An act of Congress has made it our official national anthem, but it has always been so considered. There is an etiquette of the national anthem. It may not be played as part of a medley. When it is played or sung, all rise to their feet, just as people stand when the flag goes by. All service men always stand at attention.

In the National Museum at Washington you can see the battle-scarred flag that floated over Fort McHenry. It has fifteen stars and fifteen stripes. When you look at it you realize that the song is like the flag—a symbol of the history, of the spirit, and of the aspirations of our nation.

The Star Spangled Banner

Francis Scott Key   V.R. 21428   John Stafford Smith

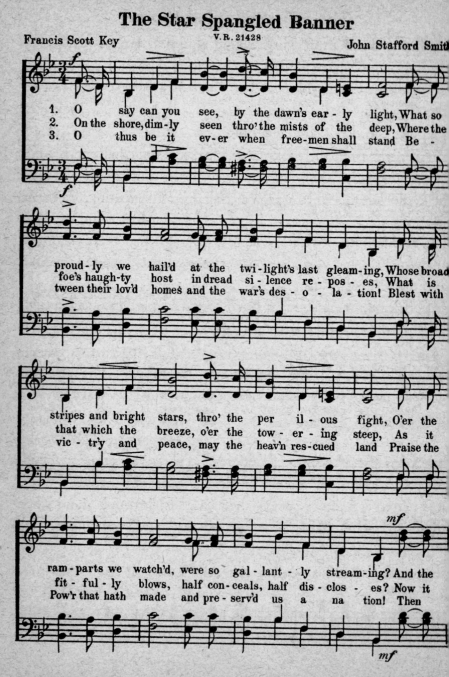

1. O   say can you   see,   by the dawn's ear - ly   light, What so
2. On the shore, dim-ly   seen thro' the mists of the   deep, Where the
3. O   thus be it   ev - er when   free-men shall   stand Be -

proud - ly we   hail'd   at the   twi - light's last   gleam-ing, Whose broad
foe's haugh-ty   host   in dread   si - lence re - pos - es, What is
tween their lov'd   homes and the   war's des - o - la - tion! Blest with

stripes and bright   stars, thro' the   per   il - ous   fight, O'er the
that which the   breeze, o'er the   tow - er - ing   steep, As it
vic - try and   peace, may the   heav'n res - cued   land Praise the

ram - parts we   watch'd, were so   gal - lant - ly   stream-ing? And the
fit - ful - ly   blows, half con - ceals, half   dis - clos - es? Now it
Pow'r that hath   made and pre - serv'd us   a   na - tion! Then

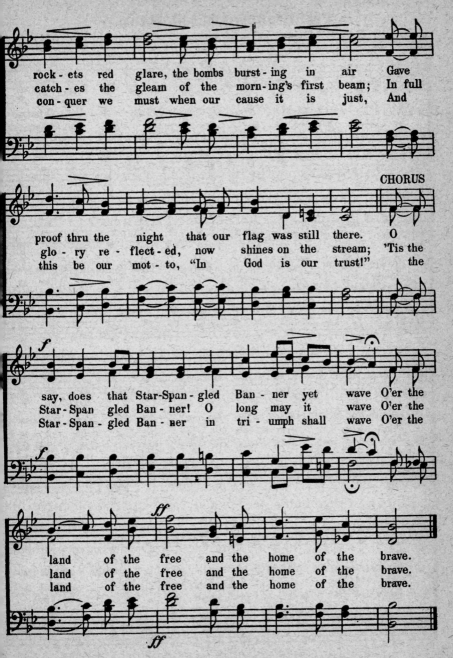

rock - ets red glare, the bombs burst - ing in air Gave
catch - es the gleam of the morn - ing's first beam; In full
con - quer we must when our cause it is just, And

proof thru the night that our flag was still there. O
glo - ry re - flect - ed, now shines on the stream; 'Tis the
this be our mot - to, "In God is our trust!" the

CHORUS

say, does that Star-Span - gled Ban - ner yet wave O'er the
Star - Span gled Ban - ner! O long may it wave O'er the
Star - Span - gled Ban - ner in tri - umph shall wave O'er the

land of the free and the home of the brave.
land of the free and the home of the brave.
land of the free and the home of the brave.

The Story of America

A little over a hundred years ago, the school children of Boston were to have a great Fourth of July celebration. But our United States had no national hymn for such an occasion. A young college student, who afterward became the Reverend Samuel F. Smith, borrowed the tune of the English song "God Save the King," and wrote new words to fit it for use in this country.

Since the United States had no king, he wrote his words about his country, about its "rocks and rills," "woods and templed hills." There is in it pride in our history and devotion to our ideals.

On Independence Day, 1832, the Boston school children sang "My Country 'Tis of Thee," for the first time, but neither the young student nor the school children guessed how many Independence Day celebrations would use their song in the future.

The United States is not the only country to borrow this old English tune, which goes way back to a Saxon folk tune. Denmark and Prussia used it, and set their own national words to its stirring music. Two German composers, Beethoven and Weber, each used the melody in their compositions. Nine other nations have also used it for patriotic songs. Even our own composer, Edward MacDowell, uses it in his "1620" although he has minor chords in the music that almost conceal it. The little tune has been used by so many different nations that it can scarely be thought of as belonging to England alone. It is a good tune for a large number of people to sing together. It has a great dignity, suited to a patriotic hymn. Perhaps some day it may be used with words for a great international Hymn of Peace, and then it will really belong to the whole world.

America

V.R.22083

S. F. Smith

Henry Carey

1. My coun - try 'tis of thee, Sweet land of
2. My na - tive coun - try, thee, Land of the
3. Let mu - sic swell the breeze, And ring from
4. Our Fa - thers' God, to Thee, Au - thor of

lib - er - ty, Of thee I sing! Land where my
no - ble free, Thy name I love; I love thy
all the trees Sweet free - dom's song; Let mor - tal
lib - er - ty, To Thee we sing! Long may our

fa - thers died, Land of the pil - grims pride;
rocks and rills, Thy woods and tem - pled hills;
tongues a - wake, Let all that breathe par - take,
land be bright With free - dom's ho - ly light,

From ev - 'ry moun - tain side Let free - dom ring!
My heart with rap - ture thrills, Like that a - bove.
Let rocks their si - lence break, The sound pro - long.
Pro - tect us by Thy might, Great God, our King!

Dixie Land

V. R. 21950

Arranged by
Collin Coe

Composed by
Dan Emmet

1. I wish I was in de land of cot-ton,
2. Dar's buck-wheat cakes an' In-gen bat-ter

Old times dar am not for-got-ten, Look a - way! Look a - way! Look a-
Makes you fat or a lit - tle fat-ter, Look a - way! Look a - way! Look a-

way! Dix-ie Land. In Dix-ie Land whar I was born in, Ear-ly on one
way! Dix-ie Land. Den hoe it down an' scratch your grab-ble, To Dix-ie land I'm

For the story of *Dixie* see page 11.

fros-ty morn-in', Look a-way! Look a-way! Look a-way! Dix-ie Land.
bound to trab-ble, Look a-way! Look a-way! Look a-way! Dix-ie Land.

CHORUS

Den I wish I was in Dix-ie, Hoo-ray! Hoo-ray! In Dix-ie Land I'll

take my stand, To lib and die in Dix-ie, A-way, A-way, A-

way down south in Dix-ie A-way, A-way, A-way down south in Dix-ie.

Home, Sweet Home

Four countries had a part in the writing of *Home, Sweet Home.* The words were written in France by an American, and then set to Italian music by an English composer.

While wandering amid the "pleasures and palaces" of Paris, John Howard Payne, an American actor, was overcome with longing for his childhood home in New York. The lines he wrote have since become the "home song" for the whole world.

Payne decided to use the song in a play he was writing, so he suggested to Henry Bishop, an English musician who was writing the music, that the poem would go well with the melody of an old Sicilian air. The play was an Italian opera story called *Clari, or the Maid of Milan,* and the first performance was given in London. Since that date, over a hundred years ago, the song has been popular with everyone.

One evening, some years later, Payne attend a concert in Washington, D. C. Many distinguished people had gathered to hear the famous Jenny Lind, the "Swedish Nightingale." President Fillmore, Daniel Webster, Henry Clay, and many famous people were there. At the close of the concert Miss Lind turned to Payne and sang *Home, Sweet Home.* How everyone cheered!

Payne did not profit much by his song, although many thousands of copies were sold. Our government made him consul at Tunis, in northern Africa, where he died. On his simple gravestone are the words:

> When thy gentle spirit fled
> To realms beyond the azure dome,
> With arms outstretched God's angels said
> "Welcome to Heaven's Home, Sweet Home."

Home, Sweet Home

John Howard Payne   V.R. 21949   Henry R. Bishop

1. 'Mid pleas-ures and pal-ac - es though we may roam, Be it ev - er so
2. An ex - ile from home, splen-dor dazz-les in vain; Oh, give me my

hum - ble, there's no place like home! A charm from the skies seems to
low - ly thatched cot - tage a - gain! The birds sing-ing gai - ly that

hal - low us there, Which, seek thro' the world is ne'er met with else-where
come at my call; Give me them with the peace of mind, dear-er than all.

CHORUS

Home! home! sweet, sweet home! There's no place like home, there's no place like home.

From "Golden Book of Favorite Songs" published by Hall & McCreary, Chicago, Ill.

The Story of "Annie Laurie"

The Scottish *Annie Laurie* which is known as the world's favorite love lyric shows how a song is really created. How many people have helped to make it! And how many hearts have gone into the singing of it! In *A Song in Camp,* the poet Bayard Taylor says:

> *"Give us a song" the soldiers cried,*
> *The outer trenches guarding,*
> *When the heavy guns of the arms allied*
> *Grew weary of bombarding.*
> *They sang of love and not of war,*
> *Forgot was Britain's glory,*
> *Each man recalled a different face*
> *But all sang "Annie Laurie".*

There are many versions of *Annie Laurie,* and legend says it has had several tunes. The one that is sung today is so Scotch that, as it is sung, one can "fair smell the heather". It comes from a poem written by William Douglas, about the year 1705. The young poet of England was in love with the daughter of Sir Robert Laurie, and in his courtship of Annie he wrote the words of our song. His lovely song, which has gripped the hearts of so many people, did not seem to make much impression on his "bonnie Annie Laurie." Whatever Douglas might have thought about "her promise true", the fact is that she married another man. Her son, Alexander Fergusson, was the hero of *The Whistle,* a poem by Robert Burns. The disappointed lover, William Douglas, was also the hero of a popular song called *Willie Was a Wanton Wag.*

The air to which we sing this song of over two centuries ago is much more recent. It is said to have been composed by Lady John Scott.

Annie Laurie

V. R. 22082

William Douglas

Lady John Scott

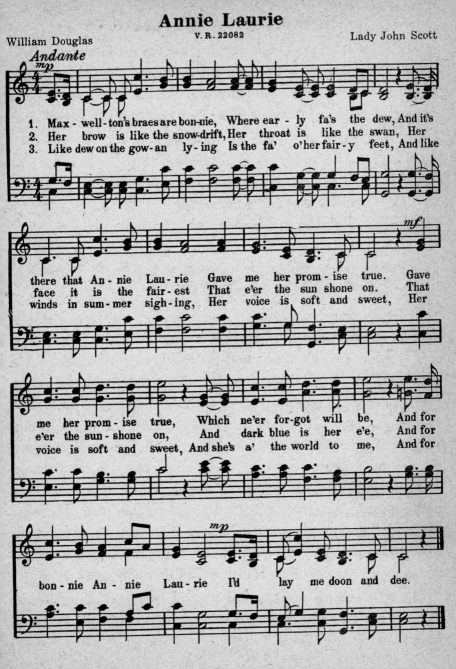

Andante

1. Max - well - ton's braes are bon-nie, Where ear - ly fa's the dew, And it's
2. Her brow is like the snow-drift, Her throat is like the swan, Her
3. Like dew on the gow-an ly - ing Is the fa' o' her fair - y feet, And like

there that An - nie Lau - rie Gave me her prom - ise true. Gave
face it is the fair - est That e'er the sun shone on. That
winds in sum - mer sigh - ing, Her voice is soft and sweet, Her

me her prom - ise true, Which ne'er for-got will be, And for
e'er the sun - shone on, And dark blue is her e'e, And for
voice is soft and sweet, And she's a' the world to me, And for

bon - nie An - nie Lau - rie I'd lay me doon and dee.

Wearing of the Green

Dion Boucicault

Irish Air

Oh! Pad-dy, dear, and did you hear the news that's going 'round, The sham-rock is for-

bid by law to grow on I-rish ground; Saint Patrick's day no more we'll keep, His

col-or can't be seen, For there's a blood-y law a-gin' the Wear-in o' the Green;

I met with Napper Tan-dy and he tuk me by the hand, And he said "How's poor ould

Ire-land, and how does she stand?" She's the most dis-tress-ful coun-try, that

ev-er you have seen; They're hanging men and women there for wearing of the green

For the story of *"Wearing of the Green"* see page 119.

Old Folks at Home

V.R. 21950

Andante espressivo

Stephen C. Foster

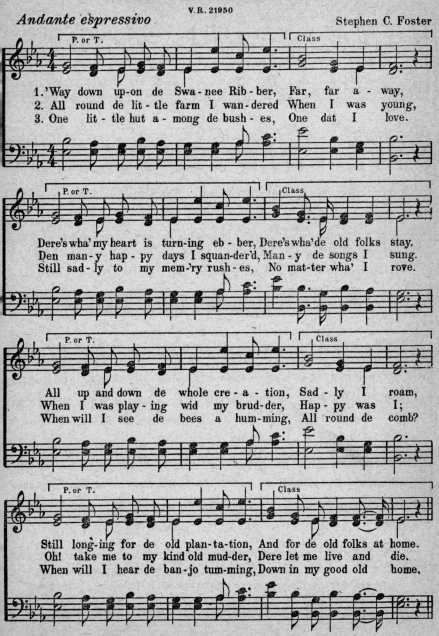

1. 'Way down up-on de Swa-nee Rib-ber, Far, far a-way,
2. All round de lit-tle farm I wan-dered When I was young,
3. One lit-tle hut a-mong de bush-es, One dat I love.

Dere's wha' my heart is turn-ing eb-ber, Dere's wha' de old folks stay.
Den man-y hap-py days I squan-der'd, Man-y de songs I sung.
Still sad-ly to my mem-'ry rush-es, No mat-ter wha' I rove.

All up and down de whole cre-a-tion, Sad-ly I roam,
When I was play-ing wid my brud-der, Hap-py was I;
When will I see de bees a hum-ming, All round de comb?

Still long-ing for de old plan-ta-tion, And for de old folks at home.
Oh! take me to my kind old mud-der, Dere let me live and die.
When will I hear de ban-jo tum-ming, Down in my good old home.

CHORUS

All de world am sad and drear-y, Eb-'ry-where I roam;

Oh! dark-ies, how my heart grows wea-ry, Far from de old folks at home.

From "Golden Book of Favorite Songs" published by Hall & McCreary, Chicago, Ill.

Songs by Stephen Collins Foster

Along a winding pike, about an hour's motor trip from Louisville, stands My Old Kentucky Home. It is a friendly old brick mansion, surrounded by broad lawns and stately trees. The house and grounds are now owned by the State of Kentucky and are a memorial for Stephen Collins Foster, America's great maker of melodies. The house has been restored to the glory of the days when, as the home of Foster's uncle, it was the center of social and political life of the nearby city of Bardstown as well as the countryside for miles around.

Visitors to this beautiful shrine are shown the room which was Foster's when he visited the plantation. A window near the old four-poster bed overlooks waving corn tops and meadows in bloom. It also gives a glimpse of the old-time slave quarters where pickaninnies rolled on the little cabin floors. Beyond the lawn, through arching boughs, may be seen the old family burying ground. Under creeping ivy is the "grassy mound" over the grave of Foster's uncle—the "Old Massa" of another of his famous songs. Down by the ruins of the old spring house visitors might see a bent old Negro basking in the Kentucky sunshine, looking like a second Old Black Joe ready for the tuneful chorus: "I'm coming." Up the winding gravelled driveway two young fellows might come, gaily strumming a banjo to the laughing music of *Oh Susanna*.

Although a northern man, Foster found the inspiration for his best songs during his visits to the South. He seemed to carry with him a constant memory of the humble slave folk whom he immortalized in his songs. *Old Folks at Home* was written in Pittsburgh, and Foster never saw the Swanee River which he made so famous. The story goes that one day he asked his brother to give him a two-syllabled name of a southern river. The brother suggested *Yazoo*, but Foster wanted a more musical name. A map of the South showed the Swanee River. That name just suited the meter of Foster's song, and so the little obscure stream became one of the most noted rivers of America.

Although Foster was the most famous musician America had produced up to his time, and though his songs sold by the hundreds of thousands, Foster himself realized very little from their sale. In povery and discouragement he lost heart, and died in actual want. His songs are often called folk songs, for like true folk songs they are simple and sincere. They are easily learned and long remembered. It is said that *Old Folks at Home* is the most widely known American song, for it has been translated into many different languages.

My Old Kentucky Home

V.R.6509

Stephen C. Foster

Rather slow

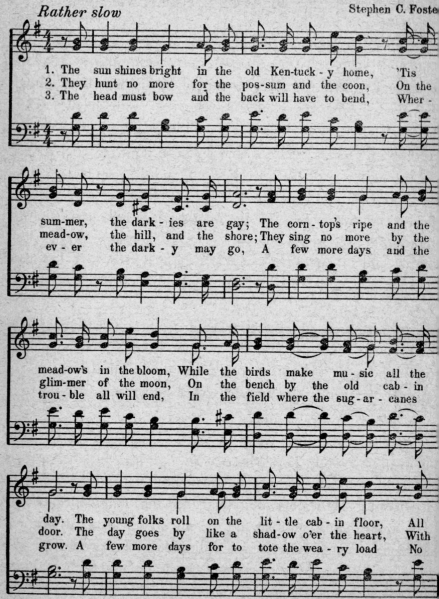

1. The sun shines bright in the old Ken-tuck-y home, 'Tis
2. They hunt no more for the pos-sum and the coon, On the
3. The head must bow and the back will have to bend, Wher -

sum-mer, the dark - ies are gay; The corn-top's ripe and the
mead-ow, the hill, and the shore; They sing no more by the
ev - er the dark - y may go, A few more days and the

mead-ow's in the bloom, While the birds make mu - sic all the
glim-mer of the moon, On the bench by the old cab - in
trou - ble all will end, In the field where the sug-ar - canes

day. The young folks roll on the lit - tle cab - in floor, All
door. The day goes by like a shad-ow o'er the heart, With
grow. A few more days for to tote the wea - ry load No

mer - ry, all hap - py and bright; By'n by hard times comes a -
sor - row where all was de - light; The time has come when the
mat - ter, 'twill nev - er be light; A few more days till we

knock-ing at the door, Then my old Ken-tuck-y home, good night!
dark-ies have to part, Then my old Ken-tuck-y home, good night!
tot - ter on the road, Then my old Ken-tuck-y home, good night!

CHORUS

Weep no more, my la - dy, O weep no more to - day! We will

sing one song for the old Ken-tuck-y home, For the old Ken-tuck-y home, far a-way.

From "Golden Book of Favorite Songs" published by Hall & McCreary, Chicago, Ill.

Oh! Susanna

V. R. 22616

S.C. Foster　　　　　　　　　　　　　　　　　　　　　　　　S.C. Foster

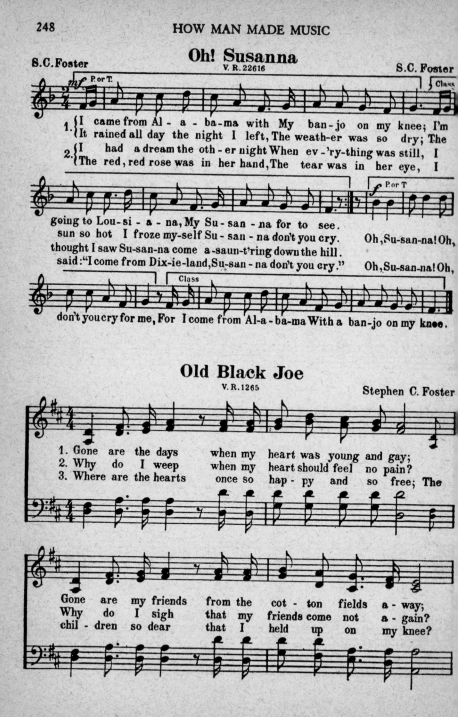

1. I came from Al - a - ba - ma with My ban - jo on my knee; I'm
It rained all day the night I left, The weath-er was so dry; The
2. I had a dream the oth - er night When ev -'ry-thing was still, I
The red, red rose was in her hand, The tear was in her eye,

going to Lou - si - a - na, My Su - san - na for to see.
sun so hot I froze my-self Su - san - na don't you cry.
thought I saw Su-san-na come a-saun-t'ring down the hill.
said: "I come from Dix-ie-land, Su-san - na don't you cry." Oh, Su-san-na! Oh,

Oh, Su-san-na! Oh,

don't you cry for me, For I come from Al-a - ba-ma With a ban-jo on my knee.

Old Black Joe

V. R. 1265

Stephen C. Foster

1. Gone are the days when my heart was young and gay;
2. Why do I weep when my heart should feel no pain?
3. Where are the hearts once so hap - py and so free; The

Gone are my friends from the cot - ton fields a - way;
Why do I sigh that my friends come not a - gain?
chil - dren so dear that I held up on my knee?

Gone from the earth   to a   bet - ter land   I know,   I
Griev - ing for forms   now de part - ed   long   a - go,   I
Gone to the shore   where my soul has longed to go,   I

hear their gen - tle voic - es call - ing, "Old   Black   Joe!"
hear their gen - tle voic - es call - ing, "Old   Black   Joe!"
hear their gen - tle voic - es call - ing, "Old   Black   Joe!"

CHORUS

I'm com - ing,   I'm com - ing   For my head is bend - ing low;   I

hear those gen - tle voic - es call - ing, "Old Black   Joe!"

From "Golden Book of Favorite Songs" published by Hall & McCreary, Chicago, Ill.

The Keys of Heaven

Old English

He { I will give you the keys of heav'n,
     I will give you the keys of heav'n.   Mad-am, will you walk.

She { Tho' you give me the keys of heav'n,
      Tho' you give me the keys of heav'n,   Yet I will not walk,

He { I will give you a blue silk gown,
     To make you fine when you go to town.   Mad-am, will you walk,

She { Tho' you give me blue silk gown,
      To make me fine when I go to town,   Yet I will not walk,

He { I will give you a coach and six,
     Six black hors-es as black as pitch.   Mad-am, will you walk,

Mad-am, will you talk, Mad-am, will you walk and talk with me?
No, I will not talk, No, I will not walk or talk with thee
Mad-am, will you talk, Mad-am, will you walk and talk with me?
No, I will not talk, No, I will not walk or talk with thee.
Mad-am, will you talk, Mad-am, will you walk and talk with me?

She: Tho' you give me a coach and six,
       Six black horses as black as pitch, Yet I will not walk,
       No, I will not talk, No, I will not walk or talk with thee

He :   I will give you the keys of my heart,
         And we'll be married till death us do part. Madam, will you walk?
         Madam, will you talk, Madam, will you walk and talk with me?

She .   Thou shalt give me the keys of thy heart,
         And we'll be married till death us do part, Yes, I will walk,
         I will walk, I will walk and talk with thee

Old English Ballads

Many people think it mysterious that the mountain people of some of our southern states sing ballads that were popular in England three centuries ago. The mystery is solved when we remember that in early colonial times little groups of pioneers moved inland from the settlements along the Atlantic coast. In fertile little mountain valleys, almost shut off from the rest of the world, they built their log homes and settled down to independent life.

Today these mountain folk sing the same songs and play the same games that their ancestors brought from England. Sometimes a song will be made over to fit some neighborhood event, but certain lines in all versions tell us of their common origin.

Barbara Allan is found with many different sets of words. It is as much a favorite with the mountaineers as it was in the days of "Good Queen Bess." In their language, it is one of the "hurtin' kind," for it tells the story of a tragedy.

Billy Boy is a jolly song-story—a joke which a young man plays on his inquisitive parent who wants to know what he has been doing. The secret is told in the last verse. "Three times six and four times seven, twenty-eight and eleven" tells that he has been visiting his grandmother, eighty-five years old. Sometimes the song is lengthened by such questions as "Can she churn a butter ball, card a hank of wool, make a feather bed, a tallow dip?" Those are occupations familiar to all the mountain women.

A Frog He Would a-Wooing Go is an old-time fun story-song. There are many old English songs in which the frog plays the part of a human hero. The choruses are usually a lot of meaningless syllables. Sometimes they are an imitation of the sounds of the fiddle which played on between the verses or during the action of the game.

The Keys of Heaven is a dialog song or duet which was probably acted out, as it sometimes is today. A hidden chorus sings the lines as the actors pantomime their parts.

Billy Boy

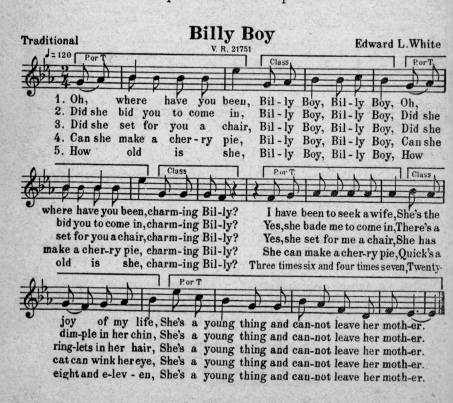

Traditional   Edward L. White

V. R. 21751

1. Oh, where have you been, Bil-ly Boy, Bil-ly Boy, Oh,
2. Did she bid you to come in, Bil-ly Boy, Bil-ly Boy, Did she
3. Did she set for you a chair, Bil-ly Boy, Bil-ly Boy, Did she
4. Can she make a cher-ry pie, Bil-ly Boy, Bil-ly Boy, Can she
5. How old is she, Bil-ly Boy, Bil-ly Boy, How

where have you been, charm-ing Bil-ly?   I have been to seek a wife, She's the
bid you to come in, charm-ing Bil-ly?   Yes, she bade me to come in, There's a
set for you a chair, charm-ing Bil-ly?   Yes, she set for me a chair, She has
make a cher-ry pie, charm-ing Bil-ly?   She can make a cher-ry pie, Quick's a
old is she, charm-ing Bil-ly?   Three times six and four times seven, Twenty-

joy of my life, She's a young thing and can-not leave her moth-er.
dim-ple in her chin, She's a young thing and can-not leave her moth-er.
ring-lets in her hair, She's a young thing and can-not leave her moth-er.
cat can wink her eye, She's a young thing and can-not leave her moth-er.
eight and e-lev - en, She's a young thing and can-not leave her moth-er.

Barbara Allan

Traditional

Old English

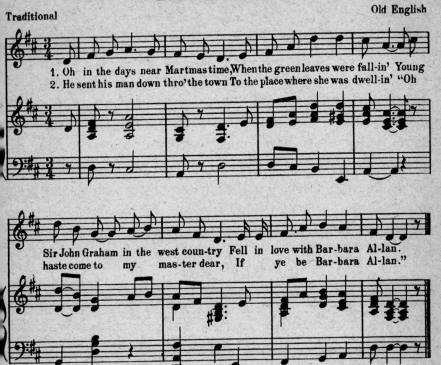

1. Oh in the days near Martmas time, When the green leaves were fall-in' Young
2. He sent his man down thro' the town To the place where she was dwell-in' "Oh

Sir John Graham in the west coun-try Fell in love with Bar-bara Al-lan.
haste come to my mas-ter dear, If ye be Bar-bara Al-lan."

3 Then slowly, slowly she came up
To the place where he was lyin',
And said as she drew near the bed,
"Young man I think ye're dyin'

4. "Its oh I'm sick, I'm very sick,
An a' for Barbara Allan;
Oh pretty maiden pity me
I'm on my death bed lyin'."

5. "Oh dinna ye mind, young man," she said,
"When in the tavern drinking
That ye made healths go round and round,
An' slighted Barbara Allan?"

6. He turned his face unto the wa'
And death o'er him was stealing;
"Adieu, adieu, my dear friends a'
Be kind to Barbara Allan."

7. And slowly, slowly she rose up,
And slowly, slowly left him,
And sighin' said she could not stay
Since all of life had left him.

8. She hadna gone a mile until
She heard the death-bell ringin'
And every turn the death-bell tolled
She cried, "Poor Barbara Allen."

9. "Oh mother, mother, make my bed,
And make it saft and narrow;
Since my love died for me today,
I'll die for him tomorrow."

A Frog He Would A Wooing Go

V. R. 19830

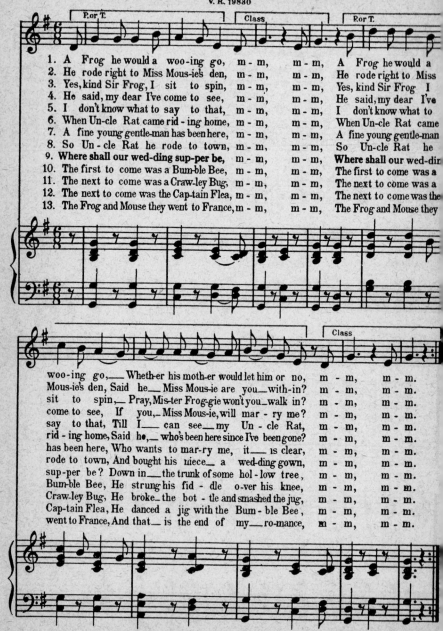

I Ain't Gwine Study War No More

LEADER

1. Gwine to lay down my bur - den, Down by the riv - er-side,
2. Gwine to lay down my sword an'shiel,' Down by the riv - er-side,
3. Gwine to try on my long white robe, Down by the riv - er-side,
4. Gwine to try on my star-ry crown, Down by the riv - er-side,

Down by the riv - er - side, Down by the riv - er - side;
Down by the riv - er - side, Down by the riv - er - side;
Down by the riv - er - side, Down by the riv - er - side;
Down by the riv - er - side, Down by the riv - er - side;

LEADER

Gwine to lay down my bur - den, Down by the riv-er-side, to
Gwine to lay down my sword an'shiel' Down by the riv-er-side, to
Gwine to try on my long white robe, Down by the riv-er-side, to
Gwine to try on my star-ry crown, Down by the riv-er-side, to

REFRAIN

stud - y war no more
stud - y war no more.
stud - y war no more.
stud - y war no more.

I ain't gwine stu - dy war no

more, Ain't gwine stud-y war no more, Ain't gwine stud-y

(bass) war no more,_____ Ain't gwine stud-y war no more, Ain't gwine

(stud-y war no more)

stud-y war no more, Ain't gwine stud-y war no more! no more!

Steal Away

An aged Negro, explaining how the spirituals grew, recounted: "When the slaves wanted to steal away from their cabins to hold a prayer meeting, the word had to be passed from one to another in a sort of code. In the cotton field perhaps a leader would sing 'Steal away to Jesus.' Nearby workers, understanding, would take up the refrain. As it rolled along from group to group, some would vary it by singing alto, others tenor, and still others might add a bass part. Perhaps at the meeting the middle part would be added by a leader and later sung by all in unison."

Steal Away

V.R. 1687

Negro Melody

Steal a-way, steal a-way, Steal a way to Je - sus.

Steal a - way, steal a-way home, I ain't got long to

stay here.
Fine.
1. My Lord calls me, He calls me by the
2. Green trees bend - ing, Poor sin - ner stands a -
3. My Lord calls me, He calls me by the

Fine

D S. al Fine

thun - der, The trum - pet sound with - in - a my soul!
tremb - ling; The trum - pet sound with - in - a my soul!
light - ning; The trum - pet sound with - in - a my soul!

Swing Low, Sweet Chariot

V.R. 24244

Slave Hymn

Swing low, sweet char-i-ot, Com-ing for to car-ry me home,

Swing low, sweet char-i-ot, Com-ing for to car-ry me home.

1. I looked o-ver Jor-dan, and what did I see, Com-ing for to car-ry me
2. If you get there be-fore I do, Com-ing for to car-ry me
3. The bright-est day that ev-er I saw, Com-ing for to car-ry me
4. I'm some-times up and some-times down, Com-ing for to car-ry me

home? A band of an-gels com-ing af-ter me, Com-ing for to car-ry me home.
home, Tell all my friends I'm com-ing too, Com-ing for to car-ry me home.
home, When Je-sus wash'd my sins a-way, Com-ing for to car-ry me home.
home, But still my soul feels heav'n-ly bound, Com-ing for to car-ry me home.

We Won't Go Home Until Morning

Traditional

We won't go home un-til morn-ing; We won't go home un-til

morn-ing; We won't go home un-til morn-ing, Per-haps we won't go

then, Per-haps we won't go then; Per-haps we won't go

then, We won't go home un-til morn-ing Per-haps we won't go then;

For the story of "We Won't Go Home Until Morning" see page 113.

Two Great German Chorals

Five hundred years ago, before the time when Columbus discovered America, all the songs used in churches everywhere were sung in Latin. Only trained choirs of men and boys were able to sing, for the people did not know the words. It would have been thought very strange and out-of-place if any of the people in church had sung with the choir.

Martin Luther, a young German monk of the time, believed that everybody should sing in church. He felt that singing was a fine way for the people to worship God. Now Luther was a musician, as well as a monk. He not only composed tunes but fitted German words to them. He translated some of the Latin choir songs into the German language. He found other tunes and adapted German words to them, also. He knew that such tunes would have to be simple if untrained people were to sing them in church.

These simple, dignified songs are called chorals. The music has strength and solidity. It is easy to learn, and is most effective when sung by many voices.

One of the most famous of Luther's chorals is found in the hymnals of many churches. It is *A Mighty Fortress is Our God*. Sometimes the German title *Ein Feste Burg* is given to it. Another famous choral is the hymn *Alleluia*. The music has been used in the German churches for hundreds of years. The beautiful words are said to be a translation of some lines written by St. Francis of Assisi (As-see′ze), who lived more than seven hundred years ago. The love of this saint for the great outdoors and the beauties of nature are reflected in this old choral. It is always sung with dignity and feeling.

Alleluia

Words credited to ST FRANCIS of ASSISI.

German Melody 17th Century
Arr. by RENA M. PARISH

1. All crea-tures of our God and King, Lift up your voice and with us
2. Thou rush-ing wind that art so strong, Ye clouds that sail in heav'n a-
3. Thou flow-ing wa-ter pure and clear, Make mu-sic for our Lord to
4. Dear Moth-er Earth, who day by day, Un-fold-est bless-ings on our

sing, Al-le-lu-ia! Al-le-lu-ia! Thou burn-ing sun with gold-en
lone, Al-le-lu-ia! Al-le-lu-ia! Thou ris-ing morn, in praise re-
hear, Al-le-lu-ia! Al-le-lu-ia! Thou fire so mas-ter-ful and
way, Al-le-lu-ia! Al-le-lu-ia! The flow'rs and fruit that in thee

beam, Thou sil-ver moon with soft-er gleam, O praise Him! Al-le-
joice, Ye lights of eve-ning find a voice, O praise Him! Al-le-
bright, That giv-est man both warmth and light, O praise Him! Al-le-
grow, Let them His glo-ry al-so show, O praise Him! Al-le-

lu-ia! Al-le-lu-ia! Al-le-lu-ia! Al-le-lu-ia!

A Mighty Fortress Is Our God

"Ein' Feste Burg"   V.R. 1692   Martin Luther, 1529

1. A might-y fort-ress is our God, A bul-wark nev-er fail ing; Our
2. Did we in our own strength confide, Our striving would be los ing; Were

help-er He, a mid the flood Of mor-tal ills pre vail ing. For
not the right man on our side, The man of God's own choos ing. Dost

still our an-cient foe Doth seek to work us woe; His craft and pow'r are
ask who that may be? Christ Je-sus, it. is He; Lord Sab-baoth is His

great, And armed with cru-el hate, On earth is not his e qual
name, From age to age the same, And He must win the bat - tle

3. And though this world, with demons filled,
   Should threaten to undo us,
We will not fear, for God hath willed
   His truth to triumph through us.
      The Prince of darkness grim,
      We tremble not for him;
      His rage we can endure,
      For lo! his doom is sure:
   One little word shall fell him.

4. That word above all earthly powers,
   No thanks to them, abideth;
The Spirit and the gifts are ours
   Through Him who with us sideth.
      Let goods and kindred go,
      This mortal life also;
      The body they may kill;
      God's truth abideth still,
   His kingdom is for ever.

Amaryllis

V.R. 24372

Fannie R. Buchanan

Arr. by Merle E. Vietmeier

Men and maid - ens join the dance With the dain - ty Am - a ryl - lis; Hap - pi ness is in her glance Glad - ness fol - lows in her train

For the story of *Amaryllis* see page 118.

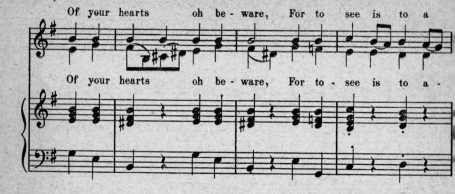

Of your hearts   oh be-ware,   For to   see is to a

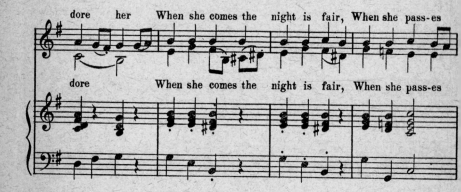

dore   her   When she comes the   night is fair,   When she pass-es

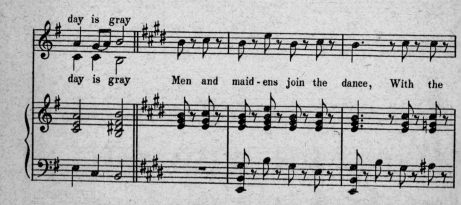

day is gray   Men and maid-ens join the   dance,   With the

dain-ty Am-a - ryl-lis; Hap-pi - ness is in her glance Glad-ness

fol - lows in her train. She is beau-ti - ful and

kind Charm she lends to all a - bout her And her

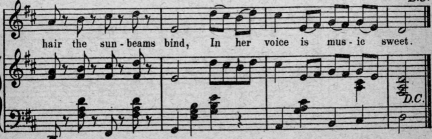

hair the sun-beams bind, In her voice is mus-ic sweet.

D.C.

The Story of John Peel

The words of the song *John Peel* take us back to England some hundred years ago and tell of an old hunter and his famous dogs. The tune is much older than the words, like so many folk tunes that were sung for years before ever being written down.

John Peel, when in his prime, always led the chase and always took the game. In his later years, unable to follow the hounds, he fell into want. Then the young men of the countryside gave a hunt in his honor. They agreed among themselves to quarry the fox and then to fall back and let Old John take it as in his earlier days. When he did they gathered about him singing this song, and presented him with a bounty which kept him in comfort the rest of his life.

John Peel

J.W.Graves   V.R.4083   North Country Song

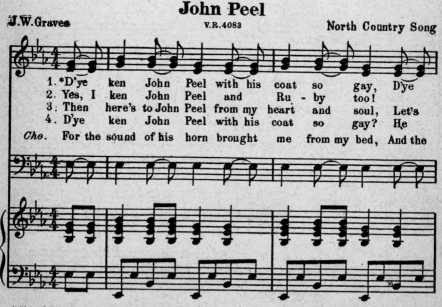

1. *D'ye   ken   John   Peel   with his   coat   so   gay,   D'ye
2. Yes, I   ken   John   Peel   and   Ru - by   too!
3. Then   here's   to John   Peel   from my   heart   and   soul,   Let's
4. D'ye   ken   John   Peel   with his   coat   so   gay?   He

Cho.   For the   sound   of his   horn   brought   me   from my   bed,   And the

* Sing the Alto and Bass in the Chorus only

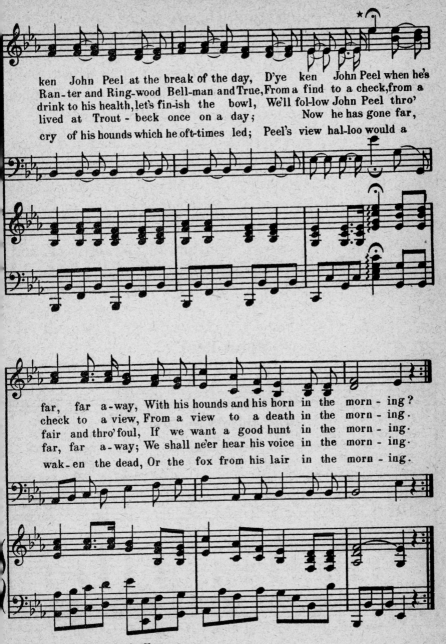

ken John Peel at the break of the day, D'ye ken John Peel when he's
Ran-ter and Ring-wood Bell-man and True, From a find to a check, from a
drink to his health, let's fin-ish the bowl, We'll fol-low John Peel thro'
lived at Trout-beck once on a day; Now he has gone far,

cry of his hounds which he oft-times led; Peel's view hal-loo would a

far, far a-way, With his hounds and his horn in the morn-ing?
check to a view, From a view to a death in the morn-ing.
fair and thro'foul, If we want a good hunt in the morn-ing.
far, far a-way; We shall ne'er hear his voice in the morn-ing.
wak-en the dead, Or the fox from his lair in the morn-ing.

★ Observe the hold only in the Chorus

Sailor Chanteys

The chantey (pronounced shanty) comes from the days of sailing ships when the chanteyman was an important person in the crew of every vessel. Whenever the anchor was to be weighed, braces hauled, or the windlass manned, a work-song with a strong accented beat helped the men to act together. At such a time the mate would call for the chanteyman. He would sing a line, then all would join in with him, bending their backs to the task and exerting their united effort on the accented words.

No wonder the chantey song has the roll of the sea in its rhythm. Now, in the days of the great steamers, machinery does this work. The chanteyman is no longer needed to keep men working in unison. Still, the old-time chanteys are sung, not only among sailors, in port and asea, but by glee clubs and men's choruses everywhere. The rolling swing of a well-sung chantey can bring the "tang of the sea" into any concert hall and make it the favorite of almost any audience.

Blow the Man Down
V. R. 21751
Sailor's Chantey

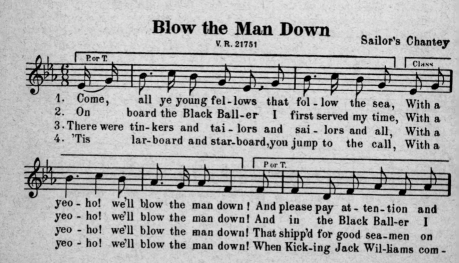

1. Come, all ye young fel-lows that fol-low the sea, With a
2. On board the Black Ball-er I first served my time, With a
3. There were tin-kers and tai-lors and sai-lors and all, With a
4. 'Tis lar-board and star-board, you jump to the call, With a

yeo - ho! we'll blow the man down! And please pay at - ten-tion and
yeo - ho! we'll blow the man down! And in the Black Ball-er I
yeo - ho! we'll blow the man down! That shipp'd for good sea-men on
yeo - ho! we'll blow the man down! When Kick-ing Jack Wil-liams com-

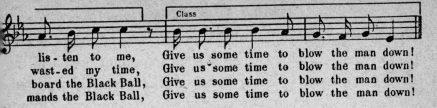

lis - ten to me, Give us some time to blow the man down!
wast-ed my time, Give us some time to blow the man down!
board the Black Ball, Give us some time to blow the man down!
mands the Black Ball, Give us some time to blow the man down!

Away for Rio!

V. R. 21751

Old Sailor Chantey

1. O the an-chor is weighed and the sails they are set; A - way for
2. So we'll man the good cap-stan and run it a-round; A - way for
3. We've a jol - ly good ship and a jol - ly good crew; A - way for
4. Let us sing as we heave, to the friends that we leave; A - way for
5. So come heave up the an-chor, let's get it a-weigh; A - way for
6. We will heave with a will and heave stead-y and strong; A - way for

Ri - o! The town that we're leav-ing we'll nev- er for-get For we're
Ri - o! We'll heave up the an-chor to this jol - ly sound For we're
Ri - o! A jol - ly good mate and a good skip-per too, For we're
Ri - o! They know at this part-ing how sad - ly we grieve, For we're
Ri - o! It's got a firm grip, so heave steady, I say, For we're
Ri - o! Come, sing a good cho-rus, for 'tis a good song, For we're

bound for Ri-o Grande. So a - way to Ri-o! And aye for Ri-o! Sing

fare ye well for man - y a day; We are bound for Ri-o Grande!

When I Was Seventeen

Free translation from Swedish
By Fannie R. Buchanan

Swedish Folk Tune
Arr. by M. E. Vietmeier

1. All my child-hood was hap-py and gay, Glad my
2. Years slipp'd by I am now sev-en-teen Spring has
3. Why these tears when my friends all are dear? My smiles

heart and the hours were fill'd with play   I was mer-ry and all life was
come cuck-oo sings all earth is green   Yet no long-er each mo-ment is
fade and my cheeks pale as with fear;   Now I flush at the glance of an

fair,   Not a mo-ment of sad-ness or care
glad,   With-out rea-son an hour will be sad.
eye,   Is it bet-ter to live or to die?

La la la, la la la, La
la la la la la! La la la, la
la la, La la la, la, la, la, la, la, la.

Comrade Song

Fannie R. Buchanan

Italian Folk Tune

1. When the lark to greet the sun is gai - ly wing - ing   O - ver
2. When the ves - per spar - row to his mate is call - ing   And the

grass - es diamond fling-ing When sweet clover breath the morn-ing breeze is
eve - ning shad-ows fall - ing. When in aft-er-glow the world is all en-

bring - ing   Oh my sis - ter come with   me.   Oh my sis - ter;
thrall - ing   Oh my sis - ter come with   me.   Oh my sis - ter;

Oh my broth - er; Let us up and out and greet the morn-ing too.
Oh my broth - er; Let us wan - der un - der heav - en's star-ry blue.

Oh my sis - ter; Oh my broth-er; I am wait - ing here for you.
Oh my sis - ter; Oh my broth-er; I am wait - ing here for you.

The Story of "Comin' Thru the Rye"

The original song, known long before Robert Burns wrote the version we know, began with these words:

Jeanie is a' weet, poor Jeanie,
Jeanie's seldom dry—she's draglet
A' her petticoaties, comin' thru the Rye.

It was a serious business for a girl to cross the rushing little River Rye on her way from country side to market. Balancing her baskets of butter and cheeses, and keeping her long skirts out of the water was a task. Small wonder the lads waited there to help and claim the traditional fee of a kiss.

Comin' Thro' the Rye

Robert Burns

V.R. 4292

Scotch Air

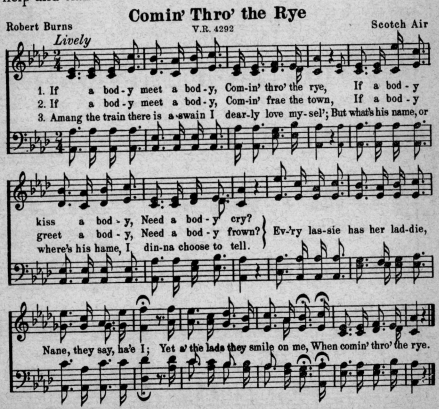

1. If a bod-y meet a bod-y, Com-in' thro' the rye, If a bod-y
2. If a bod-y meet a bod-y, Com-in' frae the town, If a bod-y
3. Amang the train there is a swain I dear-ly love my-sel'; But what's his name, or

kiss a bod-y, Need a bod-y cry?
greet a bod-y, Need a bod-y frown? } Ev-'ry las-sie has her lad-die,
where's his hame, I din-na choose to tell.

Nane, they say, ha'e I; Yet a' the lads they smile on me, When comin' thro' the rye.

Silent Night

V.R. 24243

Franz Gruber

1. Si - lent night! Ho - ly night! All is calm, all is bright!
2. Si - lent night! Ho - ly night! Shep - herds quake at the sight!
3. Si - lent night! Ho - ly night! Son of God, love's pure light,

'Round yon vir - gin moth - er and Child! Ho - ly In-fant, so ten-der and mild,
Glo - ries stream from heav-en a-far, Heav'n-ly hosts sing Al - le - lu - ia,
Ra - diant, beams from Thy ho - ly face With the dawn of re - deem-ing grace,

Sleep in heav - en - ly peace, Sleep in heav - en - ly peace.
Christ, the Sav - ior, is born, Christ, the Sav - ior, is born.
Je - sus, Lord, at Thy birth, Je - sus, Lord, at Thy birth.

The Story of Silent Night

An old Austrian tale relates how this tune came to Franz Gruber from a chorus of invisible singers. The musician was seated before the organ at midnight. Suddenly a flush of warm, rosy light filled the church, and he heard a choir of heavenly voices sing the carol which we have grown to love so well as a Christmas song.

The Story of "Emer's Farewell"

The story of Emer, the beautiful Irish girl, may be found in Lady Gregory's *Story of Cuchullain.* Cuchullain, or Cu Chullin as he is sometimes called, was an early Irish hero whose exploits have been woven into a whole cycle of songs which have been sung by the Irish bards for centuries.

As legend goes, Emer was the daughter of Forgal, who lived at Lusk, near the present city of Dublin. She was the only girl in Ireland who could talk to Cuchullain in the ancient language of the poets. Her father did not want her to marry a warrior, and persuaded Cuchullain to go to Scotland. When he returned he found that Emer was prisoner in her father's dwelling. Cuchullain leaped "with the warrior's leap" over the three walls of the fortress, seized Emer, and sprang back into his chariot. Forgal's warriors pursued him; each time they overtook him, Cuchullain stopped and killed a hundred men.

Emer's warrior husband was slain through treachery, and the beautiful girl sang this lament and then fell dead across the body of her husband. She was not the first to do this, for lovely Deirdre also sang a similar lament over the grave of her husband Naisi:

> *Dig the grave both wide and deep*
> *Sick I am and fain would sleep!*
> *Dig the grave and make it ready,*
> *Lay me on my true-love's body.*

The tune which Emer is said to have sung for her lament is one of the loveliest of all traditional melodies. It has been used for many different poems, and has also been arranged for instruments. The words used here are a free translation made from an ancient Gaelic manuscript called "Emer's Lament."

Emer's Farewell to Cuchullain

Arranged from Ancient Gaelic
by Fannie R. Buchanan

V.R. 22166

Traditional Irish Tune

Fare-well to thee, fare-well, fare-well Cu-chul-lain, Love of my life, light of my earth and sky; Death binds thee fast and leaves me on-ly an-guish Thou dost not hear or an-swer to my cry. Come, Co-nal,

wid - er deep - er make his rest - ing place, That it may

hold Cu-chul-lain and his bride, For I shall fol - low on in-to his

si - lence And share with Death the pil-low at his side.

The Little Brown Church

The story of this song really begins with the vale, for the vale inspired the song, and the song inspired the building of the church. Near the pioneer town of Bradford, Iowa, a singing school master, William S. Pitts, found what seemed to him an ideal spot for a church. One day, after a visit to the vale along the Cedar River, he wrote the words and music to *The Little Brown Church*. The people of the neighborhood then resolved to build the church. They had no money, but everybody helped. One man gave the land, another the logs, and others sawed the logs into lumber. There was a quarrying "bee" at which stones were cut and hauled for the foundation.

The pioneer minister had friends back in Massachusetts, and they gave the wood for the interior. This had to be hauled from the railroad, eighty miles away. The bell was another gift from eastern friends. It was cast in New York, and then shipped to the town of Dubuque. Teams hauled it over the rough country roads to the little frame building.

After many difficulties, the church was completed. In the year 1864 the congregation gathered and the singing master led them in singing his own song. Seated on their rough plank benches, they little thought how far from their valley this song would be heard.

Now the church stands in the midst of well-tilled fields, for the wildwood is gone. Its registration book contains the signatures of many famous visitors. Frequently the old bell rings out for wedding ceremonies, for many bridal parties travel miles, some from distant states, to the Little Brown Church in the Vale.

The Little Brown Church

V. R. 22616

W.S.P.

Wm. S. Pitts

1. There's a church in the val - ley by the wild wood, No love - li - er place in the dale, No spot is so dear to my child - hood, As the lit - tle brown church in the vale.

2. How sweet on a bright Sab-bath morn - ing To list to the clear ring-ing bell; Its tones so sweet - ly are call - ing, O, come to the church in the vale.

3. There, close by the church in the val - ley, Lies one that I loved so well; She sleeps, sweet-ly sleeps 'neath the wil - low; Dis - turb not her rest in the vale.

The Song of the Volga Boatmen

In the days of old Russia, the heavy freight boats on the Volga River were hauled by men who were harnessed, like draft animals, to the tow lines. These men toiled along the towpath, tugging and straining at loads often far too heavy for them. To encourage one another, and to time the pull at the line, the men called out the Russian words which mean "Yo-heave-ho."

After a time, this call of "Yo-heave-ho" became a kind of chanting call in which the pull on the line marked the accent. Then other words were added and the men sang together to ease the hours of panting toil. A less burdened and brighter strain of music was added, perhaps to be sung as the men neared a place where they could rest or the work was less hard.

This song of the Volga boatmen, with its chanting call and contrasting, brighter strain, has grown into one of the most remarkable of all work-songs. It is begun softly to give the feeling of distance. The tone increases in volume as though singing men were drawing nearer. The great climax seems to bring the barge and struggling men before our very eyes, and then it dies out gradually as the singers vanish about a bend.

The Volga Towing Path

V. R. 22456

M. Louise Baum

Russian Melody

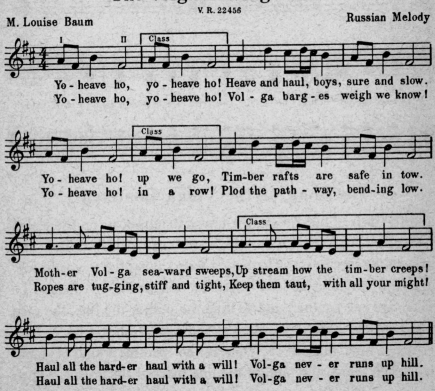

Yo - heave ho, yo - heave ho! Heave and haul, boys, sure and slow.
Yo - heave ho, yo - heave ho! Vol - ga barg - es weigh we know!

Yo - heave ho! up we go, Tim - ber rafts are safe in tow.
Yo - heave ho! in a row! Plod the path - way, bend - ing low.

Moth - er Vol - ga sea - ward sweeps, Up stream how the tim - ber creeps!
Ropes are tug - ging, stiff and tight, Keep them taut, with all your might!

Haul all the hard - er haul with a will! Vol - ga nev - er runs up hill.
Haul all the hard - er haul with a will! Vol - ga nev - er runs up hill.

Stars of the Summer Night

Longfellow V. R. 21938 I. B. Woodbury

1. Stars of the sum-mer night, Far in yon az-ure deeps,
2. Moon of the sum-mer night, Far down yon west-ern steeps,
3. Dreams of the sum-mer night, Tell her, her lov-er keeps

Hide, hide your gold-en light, She sleeps, my la-dy
Sink, sink in sil-ver light, She sleeps, my la-dy
Watch while, in slum-bers light, She sleeps, my la-dy

sleeps, She sleeps, She sleeps, my la-dy sleeps.
sleeps, She sleeps, She sleeps, my la-dy sleeps.
sleeps, She sleeps, She sleeps, my la-dy sleeps.

Stars of the Summer Night

In the days when knighthood was in flower, a fair lady was often wooed and won by music. According to the custom of that romantic age, the lover, after nightfall, stole into her garden, and beneath her window sang sweet songs to lull his beloved into dreams. The music was calm, quiet, and *serene,* and so these love songs of the evening came to be known as serenades.

The many serenades, both instrumental and vocal, which are heard today are echoes from these old-world gardens. In Longfellow's poem-story "The Spanish Student," a serenade is described. There is the lovely lady looking down from her balcony into a moonlit garden sweet with lilacs and music, for the serenader is singing *Stars of the Summer Night.*

An American musician caught the spirit of Longfellow's poem and set the words to music which is as serenely beautiful as any serenade should be. There is another verse which reads:

> *Wind of the summer night,*
> > *Where yonder woodbine creeps,*
> *Fold, fold thy pinions light,*
> > *She sleeps, my lady sleeps,*
> > *She sleeps she sleeps, my lady sleeps.*

Thomas Moore and His Bride

About a hundred years ago, Thomas Moore was living in a cottage in the English countryside with his bride, a beautiful girl who had been a famous actress. Moore was famous, too, for the poems he wrote for old Irish melodies were very popular. One day Moore very reluctantly left for Italy on business. His wife was ailing, but he left her in charge of a faithful nurse and a good doctor, promising to speed back to her.

On his return, weeks later, he was shown into a darkened room. There lay his wife, her once lovely face scarred and pitted by the terrible illness she had suffered. She knew her beauty was gone forever, and she was afraid to let her husband see her face again. Though he begged and pleaded, she would not permit him to look at her or to have the candles lighted. She thought his love would vanish as her beauty had disappeared.

In despair the poet left the room. Suddenly he felt sure that his verses could convince his wife of his undying love. So all night long he labored in the cottage study, and as the morning dawned, he sang the song which told her all that was in his heart.

Believe Me, If All Those Endearing Young Charms

V. R. 22081

Thomas Moore   Irish Air: "My Lodging is in the Cold Ground"

1. Be - lieve me, if all those en-dear-ing young charms, Which I gaze on so
2. It is not while beau-ty and youth are thine own, And thy cheek's un-pro-

fond-ly to - day, Were to change by to-mor-row, and fleet in my arms, Like
faned by a tear, That the fer-vor and faith of a soul can be known, To which

fair - y gifts fad-ing a - way, Thou wouldst still be a - dored as this
time will but make thee more dear! No, the heart that has tru-ly lov'd

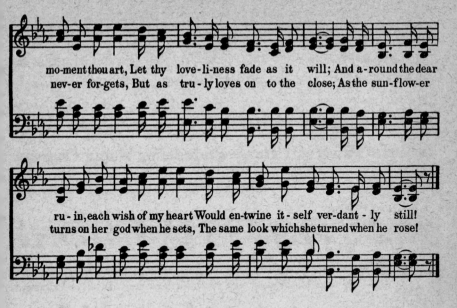

mo-ment thou art, Let thy love-li-ness fade as it will; And a-round the dear
nev-er for-gets, But as tru-ly loves on to the close; As the sun-flow-er

ru-in, each wish of my heart Would en-twine it-self ver-dant-ly still!
turns on her god when he sets, The same look which she turned when he rose!

Hark! Hark! the Lark

To Franz Schubert, the Austrian musician, a beautiful poem always suggested music. He was never so happy as when fitting words and music together. In the thirty-one years of his short life, Schubert wrote more than six hundred songs, both great and small, but all beautiful. Some of his best songs were written to words by famous poets.

One day he was seated in a restaurant reading Shakespeare's *Cymbelline.* He came to the lines where the lover sings an *aubade* or morning song beneath his lady's window. Turning to a friend, Schubert said, "If I had a bit of paper, I could write this out for a song." Finding none, he turned over the menu, drew on it the lines of the staff, and there at the table he finished *Hark! Hark! the Lark,* one of his loveliest songs.

Hark! Hark! the Lark

Serenade
V.R.4008

William Shakespeare   Franz Schubert

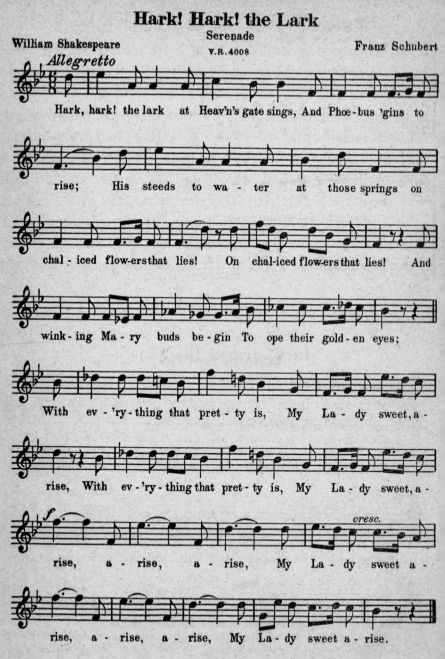

Hark, hark! the lark at Heav'n's gate sings, And Phoe-bus 'gins to rise; His steeds to wa-ter at those springs on chal-iced flow-ers that lies! On chal-iced flow-ers that lies! And wink-ing Ma-ry buds be-gin To ope their gold-en eyes; With ev-'ry-thing that pret-ty is, My La-dy sweet, a-rise, With ev-'ry-thing that pret-ty is, My La-dy sweet, a-rise, a-rise, a-rise, My La-dy sweet a-rise, a-rise, a-rise, My La-dy sweet a-rise.

English Words for an Austrian Song

Shakespeare provided the inspiration for another Schubert song In *Two Gentlemen of Verona,* Schubert found the words for *Who is Sylvia?* In the play, the lover has hired musicians to help him as he sings his serenade under the window of the lovely Sylvia. Schubert imagined the whole scene and transferred it to his music skilfully. He makes the piano imitate a guitar played against a smoothly flowing melody which exactly suits the text. In each verse the music begins softly, rises to a climax, and then dies away softly as though the lover, in the fervor of each stanza, forgets for a moment that he must not awaken the whole neighborhood. Then he remembers again to suit his singing to the moonlight hours.

Who is Sylvia?

V R. 4008

Wm. Shakespeare

F. Schubert

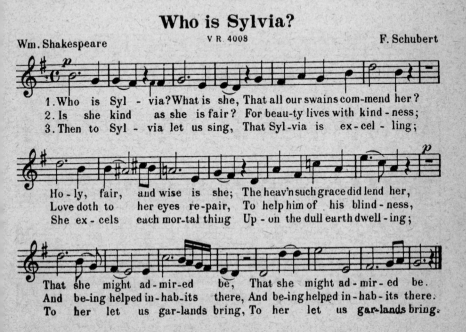

1. Who is Syl - via? What is she, That all our swains com-mend her?
2. Is she kind as she is fair? For beau-ty lives with kind - ness;
3. Then to Syl - via let us sing, That Syl-via is ex - cel - ling;

Ho - ly, fair, and wise is she; The heav'n such grace did lend her,
Love doth to her eyes re-pair, To help him of his blind - ness,
She ex - cels each mor-tal thing Up - on the dull earth dwell - ing;

That she might ad - mir-ed be, That she might ad - mir-ed be.
And be-ing helped in-hab-its there, And be-ing helped in-hab-its there.
To her let us gar-lands bring, To her let us gar-lands bring.

A Song From Grateful Hearts

When the plague called the "Black Death" swept Europe six hundred years ago, people shut themselves up in their homes rather than risk going out to be struck down with disease. On Christmas Eve, in the German city of Goldberg, one man could stand the loneliness no longer. The city was so quiet that he feared he was the only one left alive. So he unbarred his door and walked down the street. To keep up his courage, perhaps, he sang a little carol.

Suddenly a voice took up the strain and a neighbor joined him. One by one others came from the still houses, until there were twenty-five in all—men, women, and children—all that remained alive in Goldberg. Cheered by each other, they set about the task of putting their city in order. Not one of them fell sick of the plague. For centuries afterward, the people of Goldberg held a Christmas Eve service and marched together singing Marien-Lieder, or "Songs of Mary."

Marien-Lied

Traditional German

To us this day is born a child. God with us. His moth-er is a

vir-gin mild. God with us. God with us. A-gainst us who dare be?

The Crusaders' Hymn

In the Middle Ages great companies of Christian soldiers banded together to journey to Jerusalem and capture that city from the Turks who had taken possession of it. These men took as their badge the sign of the cross. From French words meaning "to take the cross," comes the word Crusader.

The story of the Crusaders is a tragic tale of the hardships of the two-thousand mile journey to the Holy Land, and of death, too. But it is also the romance of failure and of victory. As they marched, toilworn, weary, cold, and hungry, they sang. The power of the songs must have been great, for it helped them onward. The marching song, "Fairest Lord Jesus," is said to be one of the very tunes they sang.

Fairest Lord Jesus
"Crusaders Hymn"

Anon (German) 1677   Arr. by R. S. Willis, 1850

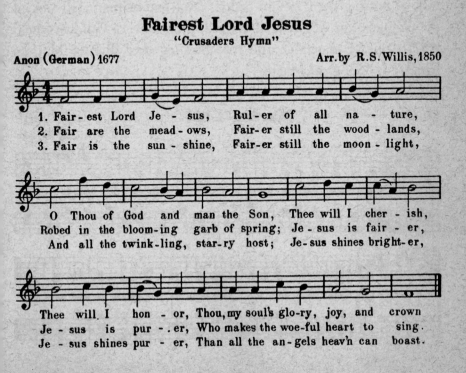

1. Fair-est Lord Je-sus, Rul-er of all na-ture,
2. Fair are the mead-ows, Fair-er still the wood-lands,
3. Fair is the sun-shine, Fair-er still the moon-light,

O Thou of God and man the Son, Thee will I cher-ish,
Robed in the bloom-ing garb of spring; Je-sus is fair-er,
And all the twink-ling, star-ry host; Je-sus shines bright-er,

Thee will I hon-or, Thou, my soul's glo-ry, joy, and crown
Je-sus is pur-er, Who makes the woe-ful heart to sing.
Je-sus shines pur-er, Than all the an-gels heav'n can boast.

Musical Notations You Should Know

𝅝 Whole note   ▬ Whole rest

𝅗𝅥 Half note   ▬ Half rest

𝅘𝅥 Quarter note   𝄽 𝄽 𝄽 Quarter rest

𝅘𝅥𝅮 Eighth note   𝄾 Eighth rest

𝅘𝅥𝅯 Sixteenth note   𝄿 Sixteenth rest

𝅘𝅥𝅰 Thirty-second note   𝅀 Thirty-second rest

𝅘𝅥. Dotted notes: equal one-half more. = 𝅘𝅥 𝅘𝅥 𝅘𝅥

𝅘𝅥𝅘𝅥𝅘𝅥 Triplets: of same value as two notes. = 𝅘𝅥 𝅘𝅥

𝄞 G or Treble Clef, locates G on the second line of the staff.

𝄢 F or Bass Clef, locates F on the fourth line of the staff.

𝄡 C or Tenor Clef, locates middle C on the third space of the staff.

2/2 Two-two, double time.

2/4 Two-four, double time.

2/8 Two-eight, double time.

3/2 Three-two, triple time.

3/4 Three-four, triple time.

$\frac{3}{8}$ Three-eight, triple time.

$\frac{4}{2}$ Four-two, quadruple time.

$\frac{4}{4}$ Four-four, quadruple time.

$\frac{4}{8}$ Four-eight, quadruple time.

$\frac{6}{8}$ Six-eight, compound double time.

$\frac{9}{8}$ Nine-eight, compound triple time.

$\frac{12}{8}$ Twelve-eight, compound quadruple time.

There are other combinations and compound times such as 6/4, 12/16, etc.

Repeat marks placed on the staff to indicate that the music placed between them is to be repeated.

Slur—used to connect two or more notes on different parts of the staff.

Tie—used to connect two notes on the same line or space of the staff which are to be sounded as one note.

Hold—a mark to indicate the note, or rest, is to be prolonged.

Crescendo, louder.

Dal segno, from the sign.

Diminuendo, softer.

Sforzando, accented.

The Instruments of an Orchestra

STRINGS:

    Violin, first and second (soprano and mezzo-soprano)

    Viola (an alto violin)

    Violoncello (a tenor violin)

    Bass Viol (bass)

    Harp

WOOD-WINDS:

    Flute (soprano)

    Piccolo (high soprano)

    Oboe (soprano)

    English Horn (a tenor oboe)

    Clarinet (tenor)

    Bass Clarinet (bass)

    Bassoon (bass oboe)

    Double-Bassoon (double bass)

BRASSES:

    Trumpet (soprano)

    Horn (alto)

    Trombone (tenor)

    Tuba (bass)

PERCUSSION INSTRUMENTS:

Kettledrums	Gong	Bells
Bass Drum	Triangle	Xylophone
Tambourine	Castanets	Chimes
Cymbals	Celesta	Snare Drum

Dictionary of Musical Terms

A capella (ah cahp-pell' la)—unaccompanied; in the style of old church music.

Accelerando (aht-chay'-lay-rahn'-doh)—increase the speed or movement.

Accent—the emphasis by which a beat or tone is distinguished from others.

Accidental—a sharp, flat, or natural which is not a part of the key in which the composition is written.

Adagio (ah-dah'-joh) slow tempo, from 100-120 beats to the minute. Also, the slow movement or part of a composition.

Ad libitum (ahd lib'-i-tum) at the pleasure or discretion of the performer.

Agitato (ah'-ji-tah-toe) agitated.

Alla (ahl'-lah) like, in the style of.

Allegretto (al'-leh-gret-toe) tempo somewhat slower than *allegro*. Also, a short allegro movement or part of a composition.

Allegro (al-lay'-grow) quick and lively tempo, from 160-184 beats to the minute. Also the lively movement or part of a composition.

Alt, altissimo (ahlt, ahl-tiss'-im-oh) notes in the octave above the treble staff are *in alt,* those in the next octave above are *in altissimo.*

Alto—the voice or part above the tenor. In mixed choruses, the voices between soprano and contralto. Also used to describe any instrument with a range corresponding to alto or immediately below the range of the highest voiced instrument of that kind.

Andante (ahn-dahn'tay) moderate tempo, smooth and flowing, 126-152 beats per minute. Also, a composition or part of one in that style and tempo.

Andantino (ahn'-dahn-tee'-no) a tempo slightly different, either faster or slower than *andante.* Also, a short *andante* movement or part of a composition.

Animato (ahn'-e-mah-toe) with spirit.

Animosa (ahn'-e-moh-sah) in a spirited and lively manner.

Antiphonal—in choral singing, when two parts of the choir sing alternately.

Aria—an air or melody. In opera, a solo with instrumental accompaniment.

A tempo (ah tem'poh) strictly according to time as indicated.

Bar—a vertical line on the staff used to separate measures. Or, the music between two such bars.

Barcarolle (bar'-kah-roll) a boat song, usually in such rhythm and accent as to suggest the movement of a boat.

Bel canto (bell can'-toe) a method or style associated with Italian singing of the 17th-18th centuries, in which finished delivery and tone were emphasized more than dramatic effect.

Berceuse (ber-suz') a cradle song or lullaby, or instrumental accompaniment in similar style.

Brio (bree'-oh) fire, vivacity. *Con brio,* with fire or vivacity.

Burden, burthen—the repeated refrain of a popular song, or the persistent sounding of a single part, such as a voice, or the drone notes of a bagpipe.

Cadence (kay'-dense) a close. The succession of notes or chords which bring a composition, or any part of it, to a close.

Cadenza (ka-den'-zah) an intricate passage in a composition, usually near the end, formerly interpolated by singers or other musicians than the composer.

Calando (kah-lahn'-doh) diminishing the tone.

Canon—a composition in which the melody of one part is imitated by another or other parts. Also, part of the service of the Mass.

Cantabile (kan-tah'-bee-lay) continuous and even, like a song.

Cantata—originally a piece to be sung, rather than one to be sounded (*sonata*). Applied to short oratorios, choral ballads, and operettas that are not acted.

Canzonetta (kan'-zon-et'-tah) a short, simple, bright song of popular character.

Capriccio (kah-preet'-cho) a composition in a free and vivacious manner.

Carol—a ring-dance or song. A festal song of popular nature, usually associated with a specific holiday or season.

Cavatina (kah-vah-tee'-nah) a less elaborate aria, or a song-like instrumental composition.

Chamber music—music for a small number of soloists or instrumentalists, such as a string trio or quartet, usually suited to performance in a room or small hall.

Chanson (shahn´-sawn) a song, usually for a single voice, often with a refrain. See also *lied*. Same as Italian *canzona*.

Chant—in church music, an intoned recitation of a Psalm or canticle.

Choir—a group of singers. Or, the subdivisions of a large chorus. Or, the sections of an orchestra, such as the brass choir, the singing choir, etc.

Choral, Chorale (ko´-ral) musical setting of any hymn or Psalm. They were sung slowly, in massive unison, at first; later, parts were added.

Chromatic—ascending or descending by half tones.

Coda (ko´-dah) a concluding phase or section of a composition.

Coloratura (ko´-low-rah-too´-rah) decorative effects such as runs, trills, graces, etc., introduced for display (color).

Common meter—in hymns, a stanza form having lines with 8-6-8-6 syllables.

Con (kohn) with.

Concerto (kohn-cher´-toe) an elaborate work for solo instrument with orchestral accompaniment.

Contralto—the lowest woman's voice or its voice part.

Crescendo (kre-shen´-doh) increasing in tone volume and power.

Da Capo (dah kah´-poh) repeat from the beginning.

Dal Segno (dahl say´-nyoh) from the sign.

Degree—the step from one scale tone to the next.

Diatonic—progressing according to the standard or diatonic scale.

Diminuendo (dee´-me-nwen´-doh) diminishing in tone volume.

Dolce (dohl´-chay) sweetly.

Doxology—in general, any hymn or song in praise of God.

Elegy—a composition of mournful character.

Energico (en-er´-je-ko) with energy.

Expressivo (es´-pres-see´-voh) with expression.

Extravaganza—a whimsical or fantastic composition like a burlesque or caricature.

Fantasia, fantasy—a short impromptu or free composition, especially one not conforming exactly to a regular style.

Finale (fee-nah'-lay) the last number of an opera, or the concluding movement or part of a composition of some length.

Fine (fee'-nay) end.

Forte (for'-teh) loud; abbreviated as *f*.

Fortissimo (for-tis'-im-oh) very loud; abbreviated as *ff*.

Fortississimo (for'-tis-sis'-im-oh) extremely loud; abbreviated as *fff*.

Forza (for'-tsa) power, force.

Fugue (fewg) an elaborate form of composition in counterpoint.

Fuoco (foo-o'-coe) fire.

Grazia (grah'-tsee-ah) grace.

Grazioso (grah'-tsee-oh'-soh) graceful.

Grave (grah'-vay) serious, also very slow tempo.

Humoresque, humoreske—a short, fanciful caprice or piece of humorous character.

Intermezzo (in'-ter-med'-zoh) a short number played between the acts of an opera or between the usual movements of a long composition.

Interval—the difference in pitch between two tones.

Invention—a short instrumental piece in which the theme is not treated elaborately.

Key—the pitch of the tones in a scale. The key note of the scales gives the key its name.

Lament—an elegy, or any plaintive composition.

Larghetto (lahr-get'-toh) slow and gentle.

Largo (lahr'-go) extremely slow tempo, 40-70 beats to the minute. Also the slow movement or part of a long composition.

Lay—a song or ballad, generally long with recurrent refrain.

Legato (lay-gah'-toh) in a connected, flowing manner.

Lento (len'-toh) slow.

Libretto (lih-bret'-oh) the literary text of an opera or other composition.

Lied (leet) song (German). Generally a particular type, written in the style of folk music.

Long Meter—in hymns, a stanza form having lines with 8-8-8-8 syllables.

Lyric—song-like and melodious, generally sentimental.

Madrigal (mad'-ri-gal) a musical setting or lyric of medieval type, usually amorous in character.

Major—keys, chords, and scales, in which the intervals are greater by a half tone than in minor intervals, are called major.

Marcato (mar-kah'-toh) accented.

Marcia (mar'-cha) march. *Alla marcia* like a march.

Measure—the notes between two bars, each measure representing a unit in the rhythm.

Melody—the notes forming an air or tune, or the leading part of a harmonized composition.

Meno mosso (may'-no mohs'-soh) less moved, slower.

Meter—the succession of regular accents which makes up the rhythm of a composition.

Mezzo (med'-zoh) half or medium. *Mezzo-forte* (*mf*) is moderately loud; *mezzo-soprano* is a voice between soprano and alto.

Minor—keys, chords, and scales, in which certain intervals are lesser by a half tone than in major intervals, are called minor.

Moderato (mod-eh-rah'-toh) moderate.

Modulation—a transition from one key to another.

Molto (mohl'-toh) much, very.

Morendo (moh-ren'-doh) gradually dying away.

Motif, motive—a distinguishing phrase which occurs frequently in a composition; or, the theme itself.

Moto (moh'-toh) motion.

Natural—a note especially marked to cancel a sharp or a flat as indicated in the key.

Noel, Nowel (no-el') a carol for Christmas, so called because they often contained the word *noel* as a burden.

Non—not.

Obbligato (ob'-lih-gah'-to) an accompaniment which is essential to the composition as it supplements the part taken by the leading voice or instrument.

Octave—an interval of eight degrees in any scale.

Opus—work, used as a means to number the works of a composer.

Overture—a prelude or introduction to an opera or other musical work; sometimes an independent composition of similar style.

Phrase—a portion of any melody performed without pause, and more or less complete in itself.

Pianissimo (pee´-an-iss´-i-moh) very soft; abbreviated as *pp*.

Pianissisimo (pee´-an-is-iss´-i-moh) extremely soft; abbreviated *ppp*.

Piano (pih-ah´-noh) soft; abbreviated *p*.

Piu (pyoo) more. *Piu forte,* louder; *piu mosso,* more rapid, etc.

Prelude—an introduction. Sometimes an independent composition of informal character.

Presto (press´-toe) fast tempo, 184-208 beats to the minute. Also, a work written in such a tempo.

Primo (pree´-moh) first. *Tempo primo,* in the original tempo.

Poco (poh´-ko) little. *Poco a poco,* little by little, gradually; *poco crescendo,* a slight crescendo.

Quasi (kwah´-see) as if, almost.

Rallentando (rall´-en-tahn´-doh) slower and softer by degrees.

Recitative—vocal declamation of the narrative parts of an opera or oratorio, usually without much accompaniment.

Reverie, revery—a work of dreamy character.

Rhapsody—generally an instrumental work like a fantasy, usually based on national melodies.

Rhythm—the metrical quality of music produced by means of regularly accented beats or measures.

Ritardando (ree´-tar-dahn´-doh) a gradual slackening of the time; abbreviated *rit*.

Ritenuto (ree´-tay-noo´-toh) holding back; abbreviated *riten*.

Romance, romanza—a ballad or song; also any composition of lyric character.

Rondeau, rondo (ron´-doe) originally a song for a round or circle dance. An instrumental composition in which the theme is repeated two or three times, alternating with one or two secondary themes.

Scherzo (sker'-tso) a passage of tuneful, vivacious character. Or, a composition of that nature.

Score—a written or printed copy of any work in which the parts are arranged one above the other to show how and when the notes are to be sounded.

Secondo (say-kohn'-doh) second.

Serenata—a form of musical work between the suite and the symphony.

Sforzando (sfor-tsahn'-doh) accented.

Short Meter—in hymns, a stanza form having lines 6-6-8-6 syllables.

Slur—in singing, the union of two or more tones on a single syllable.

Solo—alone, to be played or sung by one instrument or voice.

Sonata—at first, any composition to be played rather than sung; later, a definite form in which compositions are written.

Sonatina—a little sonata, usually in three movements and without elaborate development.

Sostenuto (sohs'-tay-noo'-toe) sustained.

Staccato (stak-kah'-toh) distinct, separated; an effect produced by cutting short the actual time of sounding a note.

Stringendo (streen-jen'-doh) hastening the time.

Suite—a set of dances in the old style; or, any series of brief compositions that have some connection with each other.

Syncopation—a change made by stressing a note that is on an unaccented beat.

Tempo (tem'-poh) the time; the rate of speed at which a composition is to be performed. From slowest to fastest, the common terms are: *largo, grave, lento, adagio, andante, moderato, allegro, presto, prestissimo.*

Tenuto (tay-noo'-toe) held to its full value, as opposed to *staccato.*

Tranquillo (trahng-kweel'-loh) tranquil, quiet.

Tutti (too'-tee) all, as contrasted with solo.

Unison—all voices and instruments performing the same part, though at times some instruments or voices may be an octave above or below.

Vivace (vee-vah'-chay) lively.

Voce (voh'-chay) voice.

List of Songs and Their Stories

(Numbers in parentheses refer to Victor Records)

INDEX